Mac and Me

LOOKING TO THE MASTER

MATTHEW SKIRTON

Bibliographic information published by the Deutsche Nationalbibliothek. The Deutsche Nationalbibliothek lists this publication in the Deutsche Nationalbibliografie; detailed bibliographic data are available in the Internet at http://dnb.d-nb.de.

Mac and Me, Looking to the Master

Published © 2023 by OM Books
Alte Neckarelzer Straße 2 · 74821 Mosbach · Deutschland
E-Mail: buchbasar.de@om.org · Internet: www.om.org/de

ISBN 978-3-947995-28-8

Cover Photo: Helen Skirton
Graphics & Layout: MediaWorks, om.org/mediaworks

This project is a joint production by OM Books and MediaWorks.

*This book is dedicated
to my wife Helen and my five children —
Hanna, Lydia, Rachel, David and James.*

*You all persuaded me to get a dog
so it's all your fault —
but I still love you all very much.*

CONTENTS

ACKNOWLEDGEMENTS

Whilst I 'blame' the family for us getting a dog, I thank a number of friends who have read through and made suggestions as I edited this book: Demi, Paula, Susan, Viv, Cath, Helen, Gill and Mum — I have appreciated and valued your help and input.

INTRODUCTION

"But ask the animals
what they think —
let them teach you." [1]

I never, ever could have imagined that I would write a book about owning a dog! After all, I have never really liked dogs, and I certainly do not consider myself to be an expert on canines in any way, shape or form.

I think it is important to really stress this point. I am not an expert on dogs, and I am completely unqualified to write a book about owning a dog other than the fact that I do actually own one. As I sit down to write this, I have only been a dog owner for just over four months: hardly enough time to get used to dog slobber on my hands or master how to 'pick up' after my dog, let alone undertake to write a book about the experience.

However, here it is. A book written by a novice dog owner who is learning what it means and what it takes to own and care for a dog. I am learning to take doggy bags everywhere with me (not the type you fill with leftover food) and I am constantly finding old dog treats in my pockets. I am getting used to picking up tennis balls that are covered in dog slobber, secretly picking dog hairs off my clothes during work meetings and, when relaxing with my family in the evening, being able to blame all smells on the dog.

There are some excellent books about understanding dog behaviour, especially Border collies – this is not one of them. Instead, I write from a position of naive innocence when it comes to understanding dogs, seeking to highlight some of the things that I, as a novice dog owner, have observed and am learning.

As I have taken my turn walking our dog over these last months, I have observed some interesting behavioural traits and recorded notes as we have walked together. These notes, which were written up immediately after returning from a walk or run, have formed diary entries, and are included in italics within the pages of this book.

I am learning to be a dog owner – a master. I'm growing in my understanding of what that means and entails. I have also, increasingly, been seeing life through my dog's eyes and I attempt in these pages to share some of the lessons I am learning about life, trust and avoiding sheep's poo.

This then is a book for those of us who struggle at times to get a dog to obey and follow us, but also for all who are looking beyond the joys and challenges of owning a dog and are seeking answers to life's bigger questions.

CHAPTER 1

What's the point?

Why on earth would anyone want to own a dog?

Dogs are noisy and hairy and clumsy. You have to look after them and feed them and walk them and train them and be patient with them and pick up after them and apologise to others for their behaviour and plan ahead constantly if you want to go out and leave them behind, and plan ahead constantly if you want to go out and take them with you.

Then there is the financial cost.

In the UK it is expected that dog owners provide for their dogs a balanced and nutritious diet, register them with a vet and keep vaccinations and worm treatments up to date. Some breeds need special grooming and nail clipping, and dogs need bedding and toys (apparently) and special harnesses and dog crates and car boot bars and even dental care. Dog owners have to consider allergies and bony elbows and inquisitive noses and long tongues. Not to mention dog slobber, sharp teeth, boredom chewing/carpet shredding, bath hating and ... well the list just goes on and on.

Did I also mention the smell?

I'm not just talking about the general 'doggy smell' in the houses of dog owners, but the really stinky smells that sometimes slip out of the innocently sleeping canine and permeate a room. Sitting in a cosy living room on a winter's evening with a dog asleep at your feet in front of an open fire seems so idyllic; it looks so lovely from the outside, but no one tells you what happens when your dog relaxes and gases pop out and the family start complaining and covering their noses and wafting cushions and ... blaming me!!! One tired, relaxing dog can produce accusing fingers and cause a room evacuation.

I have never been a 'dog person'. Whilst I was growing up, our family owned a cat. I suppose, if pushed, I would have described myself as a 'cat person' rather than 'dog person': less maintenance, more independence, smaller, cuter, more graceful, less scary and cuddlier (when they want to be) in a relaxed, therapeutic curled-up-on-your-lap sort of way.

My dislike and fear of dogs started when I was bitten by a springer spaniel during a family walk. I was five years old, observing the world through my toy binoculars when suddenly the spaniel sprang and bit deeply into my left hand. I remember the shock, the pain, the blood, the tears, the hospital visit, a poster warning about rabies that concerned my parents, an impressive bandage and the profusely apologetic owners who desperately tried to placate me and my family by offering us a puppy. I didn't want a puppy! That was when my fear, my suspicion, dare I say my dislike of dogs began.

When my wife, Helen, and I first visited the Republic of Moldova in the mid-1990s, serving as Christian Mission workers, the first church we visited was in the southern town of Cahul. At that time, most Moldovans had had very little contact with Westerners, so when word got out that a couple of foreigners were staying at the church pastor's house, young people from the youth group soon arrived. It was late in the evening; there was no electricity and a group of a dozen or so young people filed into the candlelit room where we were seated. They began asking us about life in England: "We have heard that in England people keep dogs in their houses ... that's disgusting!" They could have asked about anything, but this was the first thing these young people wanted to know. It seems that this was what they had heard and learnt while growing up in the Soviet Union – that Westerners – English people in particular – actually allow dogs to live in their homes!

We had seen that most homes in Moldova had a scrappy, filthy dog tied to a piece of wire staked to the ground just inside the gate. The dog acted as a sort of doorbell/intruder-deterrent mix. These dogs lived off scraps thrown to them by their owners and spent their days running up and down the front yard, usually caked in their own excrement, yapping and lunging at anyone who dared approach the gate. Looking at those Moldovan dogs, we certainly understood why, to these young people, it would appear to be pretty much the most disgusting thought that people would actually allow dogs into their homes.

This is not a great start to a book about owning a dog, is it? Well, I'm just trying to set the scene a little: I'm just not naturally a doggy sort of person.

After that first experience of hearing what post-Soviet people thought of dogs, Helen and I spent the next twenty years living in Moldova, working with a Christian mission and raising our five children.[2] When we became house owners we understood the need for a Moldovan 'dog security system' and so, reluctantly, became dog owners. Our first dog, Honey, a beautiful German shepherd puppy, was bought to act as guard dog at our mission base. She was stolen within a month, which kind of defeated the object. A few years later, when our oldest daughter was about four-years-old, one morning we found a sack in our garden that someone had thrown over the wall. Four tiny, flea-ridden puppies clambered over each other trying to free themselves from the sack. The sack thrower must have figured that the Christians in the community should be the ones to care for and look after any unwanted dogs, so (largely thanks to the pleas of our daughter) we decided to try again as dog owners. We donated three of the puppies to friends and within months we, together with puppy number four, Sammy, had moved into a house with a large garden. Sammy became our guard dog and lived outside. He was our dog, but we were all just a little afraid of him. He was friendly enough (to us) as long as we kept feeding him, but we never felt comfortable getting too close.

One day a small black dog also appeared in our garden. There are many strays in Moldova, so this was not completely unusual. Sammy didn't seem to mind having a companion, in fact he seemed quite taken by her; but I put my foot down. "We're not feeding another dog!" By this stage we had four children under the age of six, with another on the way. There was no way we were going to also become a 'two-dog family'. I was adamant – but my kids were insistent and concerningly persuasive. We were due to go away for a couple of nights and my five- and six-year-olds managed to negotiate a deal, whereby if the little black dog was still around our house when we returned, we would keep her. As we left, I shooed her out of our garden, secured the gate and chased her down the lane, much to my children's frustration. I hoped the little black dog would find another home and become someone else's problem.

When we returned home a couple of days later, I was disappointed to find the small black dog had somehow returned to our garden and had become Sammy's best friend. My prayers were obviously not quite as fervent as those of my children, so 'Poppy' also became a part of our household (although she was prone to wander).

We enjoyed, or perhaps better, we tolerated being dog owners during the years living in Moldova. Our dogs lived outside, never went for walks or entered the house (apart from when they tried sneaking in during thunderstorms) and did a good job acting as doorbells/guard dogs. They were

Moldovan dogs, and they did what Moldovan dogs do – bark and pretend to be aggressive to anyone who dares approach the gate.

It was when we, as a family, moved to England that 'dog negotiations' began in earnest. By now our children were teenagers and despite their negotiating skills having developed considerably, for five years I held firm. Family discussions around the pros and cons of getting a dog never materialised into action. Life was too busy. Five children all at school, with after school clubs, active social lives and sports matches every weekend, left little room to seriously consider adding a dog into the family. We occasionally allowed ourselves to daydream about getting a dog, but my conclusion was that I would only really like to be a dog owner on sunny Sunday afternoons when we would have time for long family walks in the countryside. Discussions continued, we even occasionally borrowed friends' dogs for weekends; the kids called it dog-sitting but I was always concerned when the owners called it 'respite care'. But I held firm. We were not and would not become a 'dog family'.

Finally, at the beginning of 2021, under pressure from five teenagers and a blissfully naive, dog-loving (in theory) wife (who, by the way, promised to walk him/her morning and evening, whatever the weather), in a moment of weakness I finally gave in.

Let's do it.

I reluctantly agreed that it would be lovely to go for long family walks with a perfectly behaved, cute, friendly, obedient dog; to come home from work in the evening to a calm, loving, devoted dog that would sit politely and shake a paw and welcome me into my home; a dog who would bring me my slippers and lie obediently by the fire, chin resting on my leg as I sat and read. Yep — I was ready to take the plunge. Let's do it, let's become proper British dog owners and welcome a real dog actually into our home. We had counted the cost (literally) and I suggested that by reducing our contribution to our children's university costs we could just about afford to own a dog (kids take note).

Within hours, Helen and the children were comparing dozens of dog rehoming options and we were plunged into the world of researching breeds, temperaments, dog beds, cages, leads, food, insurance and veterinary care packages. I knew there was no turning back.

What had I agreed to?

Living on the England/Wales border we soon discovered that there were a number of 'failed' sheep dogs in the area that were looking for a new home. As we researched dog character and temperament (as well as cost), it seemed to make sense for us to look at rehoming a grown dog rather than taking on a puppy.

Within days, Helen was phoning and arranging to visit farms across the border in Wales; one Saturday our girls excitedly piled into the car with us to visit a 'failed' sheep dog at a local farm.

Mac was eight months old, had disappointed the farmer by not showing an interest in sheep, and was in need of being rehomed. He was lively and friendly (a bit too lively and friendly for my liking) but Helen and the girls felt that he was the perfect match for our family. We signed some papers and within a few days Mac was on his way to his new home.

We had become dog owners!

Proper British dog owners: of a dog that we could train and take on walks and who would fall asleep in front of the fire in the evening! Our dog would be obedient, highly intelligent, perfectly trained and become a friendly, loving, devoted member of the family. He would fit in with our programme and not cause us to have to change our schedule in any way at all ...

We built a pen outside with a small door into the utility room where Mac's bed and food were set. Mac was going to be allowed into the main part of the house occasionally, to sit obediently with us in the evening before returning at a simple command to 'his' room, where he would quietly sleep through the night — the perfect family pet! How wonderful!

And then, we arrived home.

Mac entered the house together with five excited teenagers and two (mostly) enthusiastic adults. The lively, friendly puppy/junior dog suddenly transformed into a frantic, excited, hairy whirlwind. Mac seemed to think it was fun leaping on all the furniture. He frantically sped upstairs and tore through each of the children's bedrooms jumping on each bed in turn. The more the kids chased him, laughing and shouting "NO Mac!", the more he enjoyed the new game of 'how fast can I run up and down the stairs and leap over furniture and crash into people'.

I looked at Helen with a mixture of horror and 'I told you so'. Big mistake! My eyes were off the dog for a split second – both front paws that were aimed at my stomach for a classic parkour[3] move connected a little lower and as I doubled over in pain, five teenagers barged past chasing the wild black-and-white monster upstairs.

By the end of day two, the vacuum was already clogged with hair, I was making an appointment to see the asthma nurse and I was pretty distraught by what I read after googling 'Average lifespan of a Border collie?'

Why on earth would anyone want to own a dog?

CHAPTER 2

Wild
but adopted

Obedient. Graceful. Elegant. Gentle. Calm.

These are words that in no way whatsoever describe Mac.

Mac is from a family of shepherding Border collies. When we collected him from the farm we were introduced to his mother, various scrappy brothers and sisters and his 17-year-old grandfather (oh no, can collies really live that long?). Mac had been raised on the farm and was clearly used to a wild and free lifestyle. As a puppy he had been sold to a local couple but within months was back on the farm due to a death in that first adopting family. During his time back on the farm he was not showing interest in sheep and so the farmer had no reason to keep him or give him much attention.

When Mac wasn't doing parkour off the furniture and people's stomachs (and lower parts), he spent most of the first few days with us frantically sniffing every corner of his new home. I don't know exactly what was going through his little doggy brain as he explored, and to what extent he understood that this was to become his 'forever home', but those first days and weeks consisted of him having to learn what he was and was not allowed to do. At times he probably thought we had changed his name to 'NoMac'.

Thankfully, Mac had already learnt the basics. He was house-trained and would take himself outside into his pen to do his business. Apart from one small accident on his second morning with us (for which he was profusely apologetic) he has, until now, not had any accidents in the house and has never jumped up at the table or kitchen counter to try and snaffle food, which is encouraging − not something I can also say about my teenagers (the snaffling of food that is, not the toilet-related accidents)!

In the beginning Mac was frantic, excited, wanting to explore and push the boundaries – or rather discover what the boundaries actually were. He didn't know what was expected of him in his new home. Some things came naturally to him, like curling up in his new bed or pooping outside and not stealing food. But he had to learn quickly that drinking from the toilet bowl, barging into the bathroom to watch people use the toilet, chewing slippers/chairs/carpet/jackets, barking at anyone who disappeared upstairs and digging up the lawn were not acceptable. Actually, this list of things he shouldn't do is extremely long and, who am I kidding, we're four months in and he still has an awful lot to learn.

However, Mac does seem (at times) to be an intelligent dog. I reckon after these first months he understands mostly what he is and is not allowed to do: jumping in the pond and chasing fish – No! Learning to sit quietly when we eat dinner – Yes!

The first evening, when Mac had been with us for just a couple of hours, we all sat down at the table for a meal. Mac had a treat in a bowl on the floor and I, Helen and five noisy, excited teenagers sat around the table and ate and chatted and everyone kept giving instructions to this poor, confused yet excited, hairy bundle of energy.

Over the next days we could see Mac trying to work out what position he was in his new 'pack'. Somehow, he immediately discerned that I was the alpha, the leader of the pack (something I was of course secretly very proud of). Maybe it was my wellies or black woolly hat – perhaps similar to his previous owner (the farmer) – or maybe it was just that I exerted calm and firm authority in the family (who am I kidding?), but for whatever reason – much to the jealous frustration of the rest of the family – Mac would submissively throw himself at my feet and invite me to tickle his tummy every time I approached him. Mac had worked out that I was 'the master' and was above him in the pack pecking order. He also realised early on that Helen was ahead of him in the pack. She after all was the one who gave him his food. However, he obviously figured that his position with the other five 'puppies' in the family was up for grabs. Where did he stand with them? In those early days we had to help the children learn to assert their dominance, gently but firmly, over Mac. If they rolled around on the ground and allowed him to dominate them when playing, they found it much more difficult to get him to listen to them at other times, and he would then take it upon himself to try to lead and 'herd' them every time they were 'escaping' upstairs to their bedrooms.

Mac had been adopted into our family, but he still had a lot to learn about life and we were fascinated as we observed how he sought to understand his position and his identity in his new family. He was learning the rules, what 'the master' expected and how he should go about life as a part of the family. Importantly, Mac had to learn that he was accepted and loved and when he made a mistake, that forgiveness – in the form of a gentle reassuring voice and a tickled tummy, or 'tummy scrub' as the kids called it – was always freely available. He was sometimes naughty, he didn't always understand what he was not allowed to do, but he quickly learnt through a stern reprimand when he had done something wrong, and his big brown eyes would look apologetically and longingly up at us as he lay on his back and submissively showed us his tummy and said sorry.

It has been a process and in fact it is still, relatively speaking, early days, but we continue to see progress as

Mac increasingly learns and understands what he should and should not do in order to live in our home, how he must live and adapt to his new family and live in accordance with his new master's will.

> **[The Master] decided in advance to adopt us into his own family by bringing us to himself ...**
>
> **This is what he wanted to do, and it gave him great pleasure.**[4]

In these first few months, I have (mostly) enjoyed spending time with Mac. It has not always been easy. Sometimes he has made mistakes and tested my patience, but the more time I have spent with him, the more fun we have had: running, walking, playing Frisbee and football, climbing mountains and jumping in the river together — the more time we've spent together, the more comfortable he seems to have become with me and his new family.

> *The gates blew open in the wind this morning and I realised that Mac was outside on his own. As I rushed into the garden, I heard a dog barking in the distance and I suddenly pictured Mac tearing around the village, terrorising other dogs and innocent villagers. I imagined him chasing cars and the milk lorry that drives too fast through the village.*

The first week Mac was with us, he had leapt the gate and sprinted around the neighbouring churchyard, before excitedly harassing some innocent dog walkers, so for four months we have been very careful of keeping an eye on him when he is running free in the garden – and we always close the gates.

Not today.

The gates are wide open, Mac is nowhere to be seen and I can hear a dog barking somewhere in the village.

I run out onto the road but can see no sign of Mac. Barking continues in the distance, I only have flip flops on and cannot imagine running through the village with them on my feet. I close the gates and check one more time around the garden, meanwhile planning to get my trainers on, grab a lead and run towards the distant barking. After a quick search I find Mac lying innocently in the shade of a tree.

Yes, he had seen the gates were open, but he was more than happy just snoozing in the safety of our garden; no need for a frantic search and chase through the village – my fears were stilled. Mac is at home with us – he actually prefers being

*with us than running through the village. He
even prefers us to chasing squirrels – OK, so
that is going too far, but he is more content
being with us than he was at the beginning.*

*Mac has increasingly come to know us and
he is comfortable and happy to be with us.
I don't need to worry quite so much about
the gates (although we do try to be very
careful) because I know that Mac is mostly
happy with us and wants to stay close to
his family.*

Even now, as I type this sitting in the garden, Mac is lying peacefully at my feet in the shade. He appears to be more comfortable than he has ever been since he became a part of our family: just happy to be with me, in my presence, trusting me, snoozing, knowing he is safe and that if he stays close to the master, he will be loved, accepted and looked after.

As I spend time observing Mac's integration into our family and see how comfortable and secure he has become in his new home, I think how lucky he is and how wonderful it must be for him to be a part of a loving family. Mac is accepted and loved. He is protected and provided for. He is learning to accept discipline and be trained in the ways of his new family. Increasingly, we do not need to repeat instructions ten times. A simple command or even a gentle whisper or imperceptible nod of the head is enough. Mac is able to sleep, at peace, in the shade of a tree even when the gates are open and life's temptations are passing by outside, because he knows that he is safe and secure; and that he can rest because he is in the presence of his master.

We just returned from a trip down south to visit family: five of us plus Mac, in our camper van.

Before setting off we had nightmares of Mac tearing uncontrollably around my mother's garden, refusing to stay in his bed and asking to go outside all through the night.

He's only been with us for a few months and this was his first overnight trip with us, so we were quite apprehensive. Despite some small(ish) errors, which included marking his territory inside my mother's home and deciding that he should be allowed to share the more comfortable camper van beds with the boys rather than sleep on his mat on the floor, he did really well. Mac had his first experience of the beach and forest walks; he even conquered two of the Welsh Three Peaks with us on the way home. We returned home after three nights with an exhausted but happy young dog in tow.

It was when we entered our house again that we were fascinated to observe how Mac reacted. He must have wondered what camper van life was all about ... 'Sea, forest, mountains – all fun, but will I ever return to that house with my bed and my toys?'

On entering the house, we got a parkour demonstration followed by frantic barking up the stairs, but generally Mac seemed really happy to be home. As he dozed at our feet this evening and relaxed with deep exhausted sighs (as well as indescribable exhaust also from the other end), it was as if Mac was saying, "Wow, this is for real, this home isn't temporary ... I get to stay here with my master, I am really part of this family, even as hectic and mixed up as it sometimes is ... I am truly home."

**"Don't be afraid,
I've redeemed you.**

I've called your name.

You're mine." [5]

CHAPTER 3

His master's voice

Mac has certainly grown in his recognition of my voice as his master. When he first joined our family, he of course didn't know us at all. We had visited his farm once, briefly, and taken him for a trial walk, but he didn't really know us, because he had never properly spent time with us. Over these last months we have seen that he has learnt a lot. He understands some words: chickens, outside, car, walk, run, drink of water and − his favourite − squeezy cheese. In theory he also knows: sit, lie down, come and 'don't sit on my head when I'm trying to watch the football', but the jury is still out on his full comprehension of some of these.

It is not just specific words, but my tone of voice itself that he seems to increasingly understand. One of the girls can tell him to lie down without much result. Or one of our boys will try to put on a deep and gruff voice and command him, but they rarely get the same result as when I as 'the master of the house' tell him clearly and urgently to 'stop' or 'lie down'.

Mac has had to learn to recognise my voice and it would seem that he can distinguish my voice from other people's. It has taken time; indeed, we still have a long way to go but the more time he spends with me, the more comfortable he seems to become and dare I even say, the more obedient he seems to be.

I laugh when reading back that last sentence about Mac being more obedient. This morning I removed a stray sock from Mac's mouth and gathered up dozens of scattered clothes pegs from the lawn. I didn't actually catch him in the act of pulling my socks from the washing line; I suppose it could have been next door's cat, but Mac's guilty eyes looking at me from underneath the trampoline and the clothes-peg basket tightly gripped between his teeth did kind of give him away.

I just returned from a walk with Mac today. We got to certain places along the road where we usually cross and Mac would glance up at me, long tongue hanging lazily from his mouth. He caught my eye questioning whether he should cross, and I just said 'yep' and he crossed the road without me having to pull on the lead. He has spent enough time with me now, that he increasingly knows and understands what I want him to do. Today it just took a quick glance, an almost imperceptible nod and grunt from me and he knew, 'yes, it's time to cross the road'; he knew what I, as the master, wanted him to do.

I have seen how Mac has grown in his recognition and understanding of my voice. He doesn't always do exactly what I want him to do. It is taking time; it seems that there are no short cuts. However, it is also clear that simply the more time Mac is with me, the more he not only knows and recognises, but also obeys, my voice. It is still early days. He's still learning. But I am seeing that increasingly it just takes a quick glance — I only have to catch his eye, and from past experience, Mac knows and understands what I want him to do. The more time we spend together, the more he hears my gentle, firm commands, the more he knows and understands my heart.

Spending time with the master really makes all the difference.

My sheep recognise my voice.

I know them,
and they follow me.[6]

A dog called Nipper the terrier appears on the HMV (His Master's Voice) music logo. Nipper belonged to Mark Barraud and was adopted by his brother Francis when Mark died towards the end of the nineteenth century. Francis noticed the peculiar interest that Nipper took when his former master's voice was played through the horn of the wind-up disc gramophone[7]. The iconic picture of Nipper, head cocked to one side, listening intently to His Master's Voice became the trademark of HMV as a result of Nipper listening for the voice of his master. A dog truly does come to discern, recognise and appreciate His Master's Voice.

Of course, I do not think that Mac understands all of what I, as his master, say to him. I often speak to him and he will look at me intently, with that inquisitive, intense, collie stare, head cocked to one side, seeming to be desperately trying to understand. Whilst he obviously doesn't understand every instruction and only picks up on certain special words, Mac understands completely the tone of voice with which I speak to him. The more I speak to him with calm, loving, gentle words, the more settled, comfortable and even obedient he seems to be. When my voice is strong, firm, clear, consistent and trustworthy, then it makes all the difference to how Mac feels towards me, his master.

Whilst Mac may be growing in his recognition of the voice of the master, at the same time he is also extremely clumsy and rude and seemingly unaware of the size of his body. I am not used to opening a door and having someone or something barge past me and race into the room ahead of me. I have to admit that in the early days I did laugh when Mac pushed past me once and tried to race into the house, not realising that the front door (with a glass bottom) was still closed. Thud! There was a dazed look of shock (and possibly a slight concussion) as he bounced spectacularly off the door and sat on the doorstep, looking confused and bemused. I was concerned. He had really whacked into the door but it hadn't cracked, and it seemed that Mac also was OK and he appears to have learnt his lesson. I have not seen him misjudge a glass door since. In fact, Mac now has a healthy respect for closed doors (but does seem to think that by licking the glass he will be able to open them). It's amazing what a bump on the head can teach an impatient, wayward dog.

Back to my point. Our children have (mostly) learnt to be polite and allow others to enter through a doorway first, so what is it with this rude, hairy mutt? Two days ago, I decided to start to teach Mac to wait to be invited to enter a room once the door is opened.

How hard can it be?

Mac asked to go outside, and I went to the door.

Moment of truth.

I told him to sit, and he pawed at the door.

I told him again to sit and he looked at me with that 'You stupid man, I want to go outside not sit down' look. He tried licking the door – it didn't open.

After a few more clear commands to sit he walked off pretending that he never wanted to go outside in the first place.

But he knew. And I knew that he knew.

The challenge had been laid down. Who was going to cave?

Next time Mac asked to go out, I again told him to sit. He looked at me in disgust, looked back at the door and stood there. This is, I think, where the term 'stand off' comes from. I firmly but clearly repeated the command, he looked at me, then the door − this went on for at least three minutes. Finally, reluctantly and painfully slowly, Mac cautiously sat down and looked at me with a mixture of confusion and submission. I praised him, gave him a treat and he was allowed outside.

The next day, we had the same stand off but within maybe two minutes he had sat obediently (very loose use of the word obedient) and was then allowed outside. Later that day I tried again, and he sat (already) on the second command and was then allowed out.

Mac's wild, rude nature can be tamed.

He can change.

He is learning (quickly?) what the master wants, and life in our family together is now slightly calmer and happier for everyone compared to when he first entered our home. I no longer have to repeat myself a dozen times. Mac increasingly understands what we want him to do; he is growing in his understanding of my voice and my heart.

So, now for the test.

I'm going back to the house now to have lunch and Mac will ask to go outside. I will see if he has learnt his lesson ...

Success!

Just returned from lunch and Mac was amazing!

He asked to go out. I walked over and said, 'Sit'. Mac sat immediately and I opened the door, and he rushed out. He is learning. Progress. But we do still need some work on the barging!

Yesterday evening we had our first experience officially training Mac. We had a special introductory offer to attend a class in a local village alongside three other dogs and their owners. I have to admit, I was nervous. Being in a field together with other dogs – how would Mac react?

Generally, we were pretty encouraged at how he did. With one brief exception when he wanted to introduce himself to the German shepherd in the adjacent corner, Mac was pretty comfortable staying close to us.

I learnt during that first training time that repetition and clear, calm commands (and treats) are the answer. The more we sent Mac through the hoops, the more we sent him backwards and forwards through the tunnel, the more he seemed to understand our instructions. The tiny pieces of rabbit meat certainly helped, but I would like to

*think that our clear and firm instructions
also helped him understand what we were
wanting him to do.*

*Mac needs to be trained. For his own safety
he needs to be able to stop when we give
him a clear, sharp command; he must
return to us when we call him because he
doesn't fully understand the dangers of
cars and roads and barbed wire and angry
sheep farmers with guns.*

*Mac needs a master who understands
what is best for him and who leads him in
safe places.*

*But he needs to learn to listen and obey –
for his own good.*

In a few years' time, I would hope that I will be able to
report on a happy dog trotting along beside me on walks,
with perfect recall, stopping the moment I stop, pooping
on command in the right place and never chasing squirrels.
Realistically, whilst I certainly hope and expect that Mac
will grow in recognition of my voice, and indeed my heart,
I am sure he'll never be fully, 100 per cent compliant, doing
everything I tell him to do all the time, every time. After all,
he is a dog – an animal with free will – that can choose to
obey the master, or spend his life running around chasing
anything that moves.

*In the first week of walking together, Mac
and I had an interesting 'flexi lead incident'.*

He had gone one side of a lamp post and I
the other. About 2.5 metres on, we realised
we were standing next to each other, but
we could not both continue forwards. One
of us needed to go back around the pole.

I looked at Mac, he looked at me!

We both hesitated.

I realised that he did not yet understand
what had gone wrong so I stepped back
around the post and we continued on – I
noted however that I would be more
careful in the future and I expect the
same from him.

There have been times in subsequent weeks when we have
got to a similar impasse whether with a post, tree or just Mac
heading in the wrong direction. Mostly, he seems to have
learnt how to walk by staying connected to me, the master,
and he is doing better at avoiding anything that will come
between us. There is some encouragement. Mac seems to be
learning that when staying close to me, knowing my voice
and recognising my commands, walks and life in general can
be a little less stressful and painful.

Sometimes however, the 'smell trail' is just too distracting
and his nose so close to the ground, that he doesn't notice
until it is too late, and we find ourselves on opposite sides
of an obstacle. When, from my more elevated position as the
master, I see we may be heading for trouble or down the
wrong path, I give a slight pull on Mac's lead to help him

avoid any troublesome obstacles. He feels the pull, glances up, realises what is happening and readjusts his path. At other times I need to give quite a firm pull on the lead, in order to bring him back onto the correct path; and just a few times I have had to step back and haul his hairy head out of a hedge or away from a river's edge or steep embankment. It may surprise, even hurt him slightly for a moment, but it is for his good to be on the safe and correct path. I, as the master, have a better view − I can see things from a higher perspective. My nose is not (usually) fixed to the ground, and I can see the dangers ahead better than he can.

When I do see an obstacle or potential danger ahead, one thing I never do is just cut the lead and let Mac go free. However frustrated I may be as he pulls me through nettles or into mud, if he is in the wrong place or heading in the wrong direction, I am always happy to take a few steps back and help ease him onto the correct path again. I am the master; I have that higher view and can see the path ahead better than he can. I need to guide him, especially when his curious nose and lack of attentiveness lead him astray.

Today, a few months into regular running, I realised how much easier it is now. In the first weeks, Mac was pulling all over the place, wanting to stop and smell the verge. Although he took very quickly to running with me, I was often concerned at just how much he was pulling and potentially straining himself.

Mac still likes to be in front, but he rarely pulls on his lead now. He has accepted my speed and running rhythm and he is happy trotting along at my pace, rather than always trying to set his own pace.

He does like to occasionally glance back at me, tongue hanging out, just to make sure we're connected and close to each other; and when we get to within 100 metres of our house, he has taken to grabbing the lead in his mouth and trying to get me to race him, but he is increasingly running in step with me, his master, and running is much smoother now because we are in sync.

**[He] is my [Master],
I lack nothing.**

**He makes me lie down
in green pastures,
he leads me beside
quiet waters,
he refreshes my soul.**

**He guides me along
the right paths
for his name's sake.[8]**

CHAPTER 4

Freedom?!

It is now just over four months since Mac joined the family. We have enjoyed morning and evening walks together, but with Mac always safely on a lead. We find ourselves looking enviously at other dog walkers whose dogs trot obediently beside them with no lead – and do not seem to desperately want to run off and disappear.

However, we are nervous of letting Mac off the lead. Can we trust that he'll ever come back to us once he tastes freedom?

Early on in our dog-owning experience Mac was off lead in a beautiful open field, with no sheep or other animals in sight. He was happy and we were talking about how wonderful it was to have a dog and what good dog owners we were becoming.

Suddenly, Mac dived into the hedge. There was a scrabble, a squawk and a pheasant flew out of the hedge in a frantic panic, with Mac, mouth full of tail feathers, in hot pursuit. Within seconds the pheasant and Mac were out of sight, and by the time I had got into the next field, I could just see a black-and-white dot a few fields away, running crazily.

That early experience has made us very cautious of letting Mac off his lead to run free. Until he has a better recall (actually returns to us when we call him) we are nervous dog walkers and Mac remains, for the most part, on his long extendable lead. We have, over these first few months, seen some progress. Occasionally we have plucked up the courage – ensuring the field or lane is completely empty and trying to check there are no holes in hedges or gaps under gates – to cautiously let him off the lead for short amounts of time. He is mostly good, but we remain very nervous and realise he is only one squirrel/rabbit/pheasant (or just about anything fast-moving) away from a speedy, crazed disappearance.

We are most comfortable and confident as dog walkers when Mac is safely connected to us via his lead. The extending flexi lead is a simple but clever invention. Mac can wander off up to about five metres away but at any stage I can press a button to stop him from going too far. The lead automatically retracts so when Mac is closer to me there is no lead to get tangled in. OK, so we do still sometimes get a bit tangled up, but generally we do pretty well when walking together.

In the early weeks Mac would struggle a little bit at realising that he only had five metres of freedom. I had to always be alert as he got bigger, faster and stronger, sometimes fearing my arm would be pulled from its socket during those pheasant- or squirrel-spotting moments. However, Mac has learnt from experience that it also hurts him to suddenly run fast, too far, away from the master and so he now does pretty well at judging the distance and not causing a painful moment for him or me.

There are times when I see a fellow dog owner or cyclist approaching and I will quickly shorten the lead so that I can more easily keep Mac close, just in case he has a sudden desire to lunge or run. It is safest when he remains within close radius of the master.

Sometimes it is Mac who spots something up ahead first. I have learnt to recognise the signs of what may trigger sudden, challenging behaviour in Mac and I now know better when I need to hold tight, quickly shorten the lead or when I can give him more grace and freedom to run free.

The more time we have spent walking and running together, the more we have become in sync, and grown in our understanding of each other.

This morning I have just returned from our morning run. Halfway around whilst running on a pavement next to a fence, a huge dog (at least it sounded huge) suddenly threw itself at the fence trying to get at us.

Whilst my jump was instinctively away from the fence, Mac heaved himself towards it. He was tethered to me via a running harness and we both ended up pretty winded and surprised as we both leapt in opposite directions. It didn't look pretty. A woof, a whimper and a stern warning later, we were soon back jogging along again, tongue hanging out (Mac), a smile(me), both reminded that we really are better off staying close together and running completely in sync, especially

*when a scary beast tries to attack and get
between you.*

Keep me safe ...
for in you I take refuge.[9]

Slowly but surely, over these past few months, we have begun to 'risk' letting Mac run free without a lead in certain safe environments. The first few times, as soon as he realised that he was untethered, Mac shot off at a frenzied speed, probably remembering those days when he had never been restrained by a 'spoilsport master' and when he could run free and chase after anything he wanted to chase.

After those early 'crazed freedom dashes' we saw that Mac was, at times, a little uncertain and insecure about what he was and was not allowed to do when off the lead. When we unclipped him, it was as if he needed constant reassurance that we were not too far away and that he was doing what he was supposed to be doing, that everything was OK.

*Today, I had Helen drop Mac and me in
town and we decided to have our morning
walk back along the quiet lanes to our
village. A beautiful June day, sun shining
and birds singing. Mac is trotting along
beside me. I carefully look at the lane
ahead. We hear a tractor somewhere in the
distance but there's no traffic, no sheep in
surrounding fields (as far as I can see) and
thick hedgerows on both sides of the lane.
We're as safe as we can be. Let's go for it!*

I call Mac close – he sits perfectly in front of me and receives a treat.

Click; the lead is off.

Mac looks up at me and the disconnected lead in my hand.

He smiles. (OK so maybe dogs cannot actually smile but fellow dog-owners understand that look).

And Mac trots off happily and smells the verge.

He pees and moves forward, free from the lead, free from the master yet remaining close. He is happy, I am happy – and impressed and a little bit proud of my obedient dog and expert skill and care as a master dog owner/trainer.

I'm certainly not relaxed.

Whilst I think this is what countryside dog walking should be, I am fully alert, walking, searching urgently ahead for any sign of anything that is going to distract Mac and lead him off the path.

As he trots happily beside me, sometimes dropping behind, sometimes running ahead, he always seems to be checking in on me. At one stage he gets more than 30 yards ahead. I call his name and he stops and looks back. He knows what I want and he waits and lets me catch up. What a clever, obedient dog.

This is what it's all about.

It's working!

I am a dog owner who has an obedient dog who doesn't want to stray too far; a dog who always wants to stay connected with the master.

I am beginning to relax. We've cracked it, this is what dog walking should be like: sunny morning, country lanes, good exercise, happy obedient dog.

We come to a gate beside the lane. I glance quickly into the field. Thankfully there are no sheep, just wheat, waist height.

I relax.

The grass beside the gate is flattened down. Mac gets the scent of something, probably a badger, maybe a fox. I see the gate has a slight gap in it. Agghhh! Just as I tell Mac to wait, he is through the gap and is gone.

And I mean gone!

I am only yards from the gate but by the time I get into the field Mac has disappeared. That dog can move!

I shout, "Mac". Nothing. My next shouts are slightly more urgent. I think I can hear something in the hedgerow way up ahead, but still nothing.

I wonder how I will tell Helen and the kids: "Honey – I lost the dog!"

I don't even have my phone with me to call for help.

Will he come back?

Should I walk down the lane, or just wait in the field?

I call again and again; finally, after what seems like an age, Mac appears in the distance and he is at full speed, racing towards me in a dusty, dry channel between hedge and wheat.

He's only been gone a minute, but he seems frantic, almost scared. He lies down at my feet panting and I don't know whether to scold him for running off or reward him for coming back.

He looks up at me and says sorry.

Again, those who are not dog owners may wonder how a dog can say sorry, but I am learning what Mac's different looks mean. He is definitely sorry, repentant even, promising never, ever to run off again. He seems happy, relieved almost, as I reconnect the lead and we trot onwards together.

We're so much happier and safer when connected. This free walking thing is just too exciting (for Mac) and too stressful (for me).

Now maybe I am a glutton for punishment, but about twenty minutes later we are doing well, enjoying our walk, but I am getting tired of having to stop every time Mac wants to follow the scent of something on the verge or into the hedgerow.

Still no sign of vehicles, sheep or other animals so I decide to give it another try.

Mac sits nicely in front of me as I reward him and unclip the lead.

He looks up at me.

Do I detect a look of disbelief?

Possibly not disbelief, but he does look at me with his head slightly on one side: "Surely not after that last debacle?" he seems to say.

Mac is free from his lead ... and he just lies down and looks up at me.

This is not right. Mac, you're free. Have a wander, stop and smell whatever you want, just stay close and don't disappear into a field this time.

He just lies there and looks at me, long tongue hanging out, not moving.

I walk off and encourage him to follow.

Nothing.

I start running ahead and make some silly noises. Surely he'll follow now, he always wants to play.

Still he just lies there.

I'm now 20 yards away – what we have here is a doggy refusal. What is going through his mind? He is free but he is refusing to carry on!

Maybe he's tired, thirsty, hungry, hurt his paw? He just lies on the verge and looks at me.

In the end I have to return to him. I clip the lead back onto his harness and the moment he hears that click, he jumps up and we're off again. Trotting along, connected together.

A few minutes later I try again, and we go through the whole saga once again, with Mac refusing to carry on unless he is on his lead. He just lies down until I reconnect him.

It seems that today he just wants to stay close, connected to me. He just feels safer that way.

I am not an expert on dogs or canine behaviour. However, I am learning; and I do seem to increasingly understand Mac the more time we spend together.

It would seem to me that the brief experience of freedom that Mac enjoyed, his sortie into the wheat field and subsequent disappearance, appeared, at least for today, to have impacted him.

Is it possible that, at that moment when Mac was separated from me, his master,

when surrounded by tall wheat and strange
noises and smells in the hedgerow, that
he suddenly got scared? When I stopped
shouting and pondered my next move, did
it dawn on him at that moment that he
had become separated, that he could no
longer see or hear the master and that he
needed to get back as quickly as possible?

Am I pushing this too far by suggesting that
maybe, just maybe, Mac was refusing to be
set free a second time because he didn't
want to stray again? Is it that he knew that
he was just one tempting scent, one gap
in the hedge away from excitement yes,
but also separation and potential fear and
danger, and upsetting the master?

For the rest of the walk, Mac was happiest
on his flexi lead. He knew I was close; he
knew that it was best not to stray and that
he could not get lost if he remained close
and connected to the master.

Whenever Mac sees a car or any fast-moving large vehicle,
he tends to lie down in a tense 'about to pounce' sort of pose.
If he thinks the car is coming too close to him then he has
a tendency to lunge at it, which means that I, the master,
need to always be alert and ready to hold him back just in
case his natural lunging instinct kicks in and he pulls himself
into danger.

*Today as we walked along a country lane,
we both heard the noise of a car behind us.
We positioned ourselves safely on the verge
and waited for the car to pass.*

*Mac was clearly nervous. He hit the deck,
entering 'sniper mode', all senses fully alert,
ready to pounce and protect us both, if
necessary, from the noisy metal monster.*

*I kept the lead fairly tight because I'm
used to him lurching towards cars when
they go by.*

*As the car passed, I gave a gentle pull on
the lead. It was the faintest tug, just to
reassure Mac that I'm holding him, that
I am here, that he doesn't need to be
scared or lunge suddenly, even though
a car is passing by too close for comfort.*

*That slight imperceptible little tug made all
the difference and Mac didn't lunge.*

*We continue to see progress with Mac in
this area of uncontrollable lunges at cars
because he is learning. It seems that Mac,
when he feels the gentle pull of the master,
is reminded that he doesn't need to lunge
and try to protect himself – that he is safe.*

"Mac, you don't need to be afraid when you stay close to me, because I am holding you tight; when we're close everything is OK!"

**But as for me,
it is good to be near
[the Master].**

**I have made [him]
my refuge; [10]**

CHAPTER 5

The (im)perfect master

"Helen, your dog is going crazy again!" I shout from the lounge.

The football is on the TV, my feet are resting comfortably on the coffee table, and 'Helen's dog' is disturbing me, driving me crazy with his incessant barking.

It sounded like Mac was running up and down the hallway, probably switching between chewing the carpet and jumping frantically at the banister, trying to get upstairs.

It's amazing how quickly Mac becomes 'Helen's dog' when he is mischievous or disobedient, but he is of course 'my dog' when we are enjoying a beautiful sunny walk together and all is well.

I'm not proud of this.

It may have become a bit of a joke in our family, but it is this sort of thing that has led me to increasingly recognise my own imperfections as Mac's master and indeed, to my shame, as a human being. Owning a dog was supposed to be a fun and rewarding experience. It was never meant to force me into introspection and soul-searching. Having a dog was never meant to lead me on a journey of discovering more about myself, my own temperament, character flaws and tendency to laziness and selfishness.

Welcoming a dog into our home was one thing. I never realised he would come with a mirror.

Mac has just turned one year old and has been with us for four months. Whilst we are

*fairly encouraged with his progress, he still
has a lot to learn – and so do I as his master.*

*When we took him to his one dog training
session, I was challenged by the repetitive
nature of the training. The use of treats
as rewards and the way that the dogs
seemed to enjoy learning simple exercises
and commands was, I admit, impressive.
However, I'm not sure about Mac but I soon
got bored by it all, having to repeat the
same things over and over again.*

*I was impatient to see results and just
wanted 'the short cut'. But there wasn't one.*

*It seems that masters need so much
patience in order to train their dogs.*

As a dog owner, I am learning that one of my biggest
problems is patience – or rather, lack of it. I naively thought
that within a few weeks of Mac being part of our family,
we would start to have an obedient and well-behaved dog.
A firm but gentle hand, a few well-placed doggy treats and
Mac would soon turn his back on his errant, wild, formative
months and quickly become a mature, faithful and obedient
dog. Of course, I knew it would actually take time, but I didn't
quite grasp how much time and patience would be needed to
help Mac understand and learn what is expected of him as a
part of our family.

It seems that the first six months of Mac's life, together
with generations of collie breeding in his genes, have formed

in him deeply ingrained behavioural traits that take time and patience to address, if they are going to be tempered.

Mac seems to have quite a stubborn, independent streak – surely not something reflected in his master? He seems to alternate between throwing himself at my feet, asking for a tummy scrub as a lovely, engaging, playful, member of the family and at other times being a crazed, energetic, stubborn, disobedient monster. In fact, he seems to act like a stereotypical teenager.

You would think that having raised (and still in the process of raising) five teenagers, I would be well equipped to deal with an unruly, teenage dog, but the experiences of the last months have at times severely stretched me.

My children have grown up knowing to recognise at times their father's stern look. 'The look', as it has become known, is the quick stern glance they get from me when they've done something wrong or are about to. It may be a silly, unnecessary comment to a sibling, an excuse made instead of helping to clear the table after a meal, or just a general self-centred 'teenagery'-type attitude. I find 'the look' to be especially helpful when guests are with us and it would be embarrassing to have to address an issue verbally in front of them. My kids know 'the look' and what it means, because they know my heart and the expectation and desire for us to live somewhat in peace and harmony in our family. 'The look' is a helpful tool in the arsenal of a parent of teenagers. However, from experience I would add that 'the look' does not work quite so well on one's wife.

I have been encouraged to see that Mac also has learnt what 'the look' means.

Yesterday evening Mac was jumping up, nipping at one of the children. He was just playing, but his teeth are sharper than he realises and his fun was starting to become just a little bit too aggressive. I called Mac's name; he stopped his playful dancing, jumping around and I caught his eye. He got 'the look'. It was as if he shrunk, as with head down he hit the deck and lay down submissively. I just couldn't leave him like that, he seemed so sad and apologetic, repentant even. As I walked across the room towards him, he rolled onto his back, pleading with me to tickle his tummy. The look in his eyes said, "Sorry Dad, I really don't want to upset you, I promise I won't do it again. Now how about a tummy scrub?"

Whilst 'the look' often works, I've found that at times Mac needs an additional firm, strong reprimand. He needs to know and understand who is in charge and receive guidance. He sometimes needs a stern word, so that he fully grasps that certain behaviour is unacceptable. A slight tonal change in voice accompanied by 'the look' are usually enough to stop him in his tracks and make him think twice about his behaviour, roll onto his back and submissively offer me his tummy.

There is no 'return to sender' clause in our understanding with the farmer we bought Mac from (I know because I checked). Mac is with us, permanently adopted into our family and we have the responsibility to care for, protect and help him to grow and develop into a healthy, happy and fulfilled adult dog. I, as his new master, need patience to teach him, give him time to learn and I'm realising that I should not expect instant results. It is a process, with few, if any, short cuts. Probably Mac will still be learning into doggy old age (although there is that saying about old dogs and new tricks). Mac will never be perfect, and I will never be the perfect master. I struggle to be patient, I can be lazy, I do not always want to take him out for a walk or give him attention or throw slobbery tennis balls for him. There's that mirror again that Mac seems to have come with. I recognise that I can really be quite self-centred, lazy and impatient at times, although I have also been surprised by other feelings I have felt as Mac's master recently.

Today, whilst on our morning run, Mac and I got attacked by two other dogs. Well, not actually attacked, and we're not exactly talking Dobermann pinschers either, but a couple of little yappy Scottie/corgi types came running out from their driveway and woofed at us as we jogged past.

Mac is probably twice the size of these dogs and I am sure could have eaten them for breakfast, but he is really just a big hairy softie. As the two fluff balls yapped at us, Mac started whimpering and hopping around. He seemed really upset and I encouraged him to keep going. Surely we could outrun these two short-legged yappers.

As Mac became more distressed, the more I felt, as his owner, a strong urge to protect

*and look after him. I didn't want to hurt
the other two dogs, but I did want to shield
Mac from them. They were upsetting him,
scaring him. If anyone had been around,
I may have been a little embarrassed at
how wimpy and scared a big good-looking
dog like Mac was; but mostly I just wanted
to protect my dog, get him out of trouble,
keep him close to me, tickle his ears and tell
him everything was going to be alright.*

**Though I walk in the midst of
trouble, You will revive me;**

**You will stretch out Your
hand against the wrath of my
enemies, and Your right hand
will save me.**[11]

As Mac's master I'm always on the alert, looking out for other dogs, cars, any fast-moving thing and of course s-q-u-i-r-r-e-l-s; basically, anything that could suddenly distract him and lead him astray. When he's off the lead, Mac is free and seemingly without a care; I on the other hand feel a deeper sense of responsibility and feel the need to be especially vigilant. He could choose to run anywhere and do anything. He could easily get himself into trouble and so I am constantly looking out. Maybe I don't fully trust at this early stage that he's going to come back to me, that he's going to be able to look after himself. Maybe when he's more mature I'll be able to trust him more and I'll be more relaxed, but I don't know him well enough yet and he doesn't know me enough and so I am constantly on alert because I want to keep him out of trouble.

Mac is happiest trotting along with me down a country lane, being allowed to stop and smell the verge and explore the hedgerow. However, too often when we are out walking or running, I am in a hurry. Sometimes I get impatient: why does Mac feel the need to stop at every single little smell? Come on, boy, we need to finish this walk and get on with our busy lives!

> *Walking with Mac this morning I was distracted. As we walked, I was writing a text message and my mind was a million miles away. I walked, head down, eyes fixated on my little screen and at one stage I realised that Mac had stopped. He just sat there and looked at me, gazing intently at me. I had been far away, concentrating on my phone and I hadn't been talking with him or giving him any attention.*
>
> *He sat there and seemingly did not want to continue with our walk unless I was giving him my full attention. It was as if he was saying, "Dad, this is no fun without you fully present with me. Come on, leave that bright flashy thing in your pocket and let's explore together. Wow, did you smell that?! Come on, give me your attention, I don't want to do this on my own, it's just not as much fun!"*

I realise that this may sound like I am reading far too much into the reason why Mac sat, and didn't want to carry on without me. However, once I had popped my phone back into my pocket and said, "Come on boy, let's go," Mac leapt up and trotted off happily again. It really did seem that he wanted my attention. He didn't just want to go through the motions of a walk, but he actually wanted me to be fully present with him, to give him my attention, to truly be with him and to join him in his walk.

Draw near
to [the Master] and he will
draw near to you.[12]

Writing about my experiences with Mac in this chapter has caused me to recognise something of my weaknesses and failings as his master. Whilst I may not always meet the expectations and job description of what I am imagining is the 'perfect' master, I suppose I am learning more what that 'perfect' master should, in theory, be like.

I reflect upon this and find myself thinking how wonderful it must be for Mac to have been adopted into our family. I remember the skinny, slightly wild dog we first met on the farm, and I look now at the healthy, fit, handsome, obedient (mostly) dog that Mac has become. Even though he seemingly may not always show appreciation, he was chosen and has been adopted into a new family. Since that first day, I have observed a slow but sure transformation in Mac as he increasingly understands what is expected of him with his new master. As his master, I feel and recognise that sense of responsibility to look after him. To feed, protect, provide for and look out for him; to do things for his good, for his well-being, and yet I realise how far from perfect I am as Mac's master.

Through my failings as a dog owner, I increasingly see and recognise what a good, perfect master should do and be: always patient, always kind, always fully present and alert, always protecting and trusting, always persevering whilst steadily, calmly, lovingly guiding and leading.

Now that's what I would love to be like as Mac's master.

But also, that's just the sort of master I recognise I need and want to lead me in my life.

CHAPTER 6

Looking like me?

Have you ever googled 'dog owners who look like their dogs'? Well, if you haven't, I'm sure you'll give it a try now!

Like me, you have probably just wasted quite a lot of time being amused at some of the pictures online. However, I see that there are also some very interesting articles that claim it is a 'scientific fact' that dogs look like their owners and that often people can spot which dog belongs to which person due to a physical resemblance. So, is there any truth in this common claim that dog owners do tend to look like their dogs?

It is sometimes suggested that we as people are drawn towards, or attracted to, other people who bear a resemblance to ourselves.[13] So maybe we shouldn't be surprised that we also can be more likely drawn to dogs that in one way or another we may slightly resemble. An illustration of this would be, for example, where studies have shown that women with long hair are more likely to own a dog with long floppy ears.[14] It seems there may well be some truth to the suggestion that we demonstrate some sort of narcissistic tendency in being subconsciously drawn to dogs that resemble us in some way.

In addition, studies suggest that dog owners are not only attracted to dogs that resemble themselves physically, but that dogs can tend to mirror the nature, temperament or personality of their owners.[15] For example, the more a dog lives in a calm, patient environment, the calmer and more patient they may become, whilst the more a dog is subjected to anger, arguments and chaos, it makes sense that the more agitated, stressed and restless they will be. It has also been shown that similar levels of a stress hormone, cortisol, are found in owners as in their dogs, suggesting that dogs really do begin to act and share the temperament of their owners, even if they may not always share physical similarities.

We did some research before buying a Border collie. We wanted a dog that had plenty of energy (how crazy were we?), that would love long walks and accompany us on our morning runs; a dog that would fit in well with our active family life. One friend, when hearing that we were looking for a collie asked: "What about all the endless energy and exercise?" and I replied that any dog joining our family would just have to learn to adapt and keep up.

I do not feel that I particularly look like Mac, but I am seeing that, firstly, the more time Mac spends with us, the more he adapts to our lifestyle and learns to adapt to our rhythm of life; and secondly, I do recognise that there are a number of traits in Border collies that I can relate to, that to some degree I see reflected in me.

Mac is learning to fit in with our family, our lifestyle, our way of doing things. He no longer runs wild and free around a farm all day, but understands that a morning run tethered to the master is followed by enforced rest and then another walk and some more fun later in the day when everyone comes home from work/school. He is learning the importance of family mealtimes, and the expectation to sit quietly during those times. He is even having to learn that evenings in front of the TV are not a time for practising parkour off unsuspecting stomachs, however much fun that may be. And weekends? Well, there is always so much going on and so many more people around in the house. Weekends mean special times with the whole family in the garden – lots of walks and fun and interaction and frisbee!

As I write this, it is only a few days before our two oldest daughters head off (back) to their universities. The weekend has been hectic with packing, boxes, financial discussions, stress, mess everywhere and friends visiting. On Saturday evening nine extra teenagers joined our five and ... well let's just say the house felt quite full and noisy.

Mac fortunately slept peacefully through the whole evening – occasionally opening an eye as someone tickled his ears, but happy to just relax and allow the world to pass him by.

Not!!!

Mac became almost uncontrollable! After all, nine new, energetic young people had come to his house to visit and play with him. The poor dog was so excited and switched on that he reverted to his old ways and became wild again: jumping, licking, wagging, barking, herding – what fun (for him!).

We certainly see that a hectic, noisy, wild household is reflected in our dog. Mac is so much easier to control in a calm, settled environment.

I am unsure as to how much I look like my dog, and I am uncertain as to how much we, consciously or not, chose a dog that reflects my / our personality and lifestyle. However, I do see that the more time we spend together, Mac increasingly learns to reflect the lifestyle, rhythm, temperament, and maybe to some degree, the personality of his master.

... fix your attention on [the Master].

You'll be changed from the inside out.

Readily recognise what he wants from you, and quickly respond to it.[16]

It is said that Border collies are one of the most intelligent breeds of dog. There have been times in these last months when I have questioned this. Spending time with Mac has made me wonder at times, that if he is supposed to be on the more intelligent end of the canine spectrum, well, just how dumb some other dogs must be!

First case for the defence — he never switches off.

There are times when we are playing and I can tell he is getting too hot, frantically chasing every ball that runs loose in football, or running after stray tennis balls over and over again, panting like crazy — so switched on, fixated, and clearly on the edge of overdoing it.

At these times we stop: "Let's all have a break. Come on Mac, drink some water and chill out a bit."

Will he stop? Absolutely not!

As long as the ball is visible, Mac remains in 'action mode', refusing a water break. Clearly, he suffers from FOMO (Fear Of Missing Out): 'If I stop for water, they may play without me, and I'll miss out!' 'That ball may just start moving on its own and I need to be ready to stop it and prevent it from escaping.'

A similar thing happens when, in the evening, there are a few of us in the living room, and others are up and down the stairs, moving between doing homework and grazing in the kitchen. During these 'busy' times when different people are in different places, Mac just cannot settle and is desperate for the herd or pack to all be safely grouped together. When he hears the bathroom door open, he will fly to the door, crashing into it as it is closed and locked. It then becomes his duty to guard, lick and generally linger outside the door until whoever is inside emerges. This can be disconcerting for guests as when people try to leave, Mac likes to push past and enter, just to check out exactly what has been happening in the little room with all sorts of interesting smells. He feels, it seems, that he has to have his nose in everything (literally) and will not fully rest until his master and the whole family are settled down in one room. Apparently our experience, from talking with other collie owners, is fairly typical. Border collies are super task oriented, never resting until the job is done, desperate to keep everyone together, tending to be workaholics, working, working, working until they flop, exhausted and let out a huge sigh (often from both ends simultaneously).

Oh dear! I've just reread that last sentence.

Those breed or personality traits I see in Mac all sound uncomfortably familiar to me (apart from the two-directional 'sighing' of course!). I am challenged as I consider my own life whilst reflecting on Mac and his seeming inability to pace himself, to stop and rest and be still when a lot is going on around him. I wonder how often I truly switch off and can simply be still, especially in the midst of the busyness of modern life in the digital age? I reflect upon just how easily I can become distracted. There is always so much happening at work: so many meetings, so many emails to deal with, constantly juggling all sorts of responsibilities. Then there are the jobs to be done around the house and garden, social media, or news items to be caught up on and family-related issues to consider. Trying to balance and keep on top of all this means that I often find it very difficult to fully stop, switch off and completely rest and relax. It may not be the click of the bathroom door that is my trigger but how about the notification of a social media posting or that little digital envelope sign that shows I have unread emails in my inbox? I just cannot control myself: I simply must keep going and find it so difficult to stop and just be quiet and still. Too often I'm distracted. There is always so much going on that I have to 'jump up and go running crazily to the bathroom door and give it a good lick' – because something is happening and I cannot rest and be still and allow it to happen without me. I just don't want to miss out on anything.

When we let Mac become too wired and hyper, he will sometimes need a firm but gentle hand to help him lie down, to rest and stop panting, just to be calm and at peace. Sometimes I have to sit with Mac, attach his lead to his collar, and actually gently push him down, helping him to lie still. I tickle his ears and under his chin and speak gently to him. He looks deep into my eyes, almost asking for permission to stop: 'Master, can I really just stop? Are you sure I don't need to keep running around the garden, stopping pigeons from landing on the trees?' Gradually I see how he settles, and then with that massive doggy sigh he just gives in and relaxes and zonks out — until of course the slightest sound or movement means it's time to race to the bathroom and launch himself at the door once again!

I recognise and can identify to some extent with this problem of FOMO[17]: the insatiable desire, the compulsion or irresistible urge to constantly be connected, to not miss out on anything and to keep going and going. Would I not also benefit from the firm hand of a master on me? Do I need a reassuring hand to settle me, even hold me down for my own good, to protect me from myself, a hand that gently forces me to rest and just to be? Wouldn't it be wonderful to have a master who would stand over me, understand where I am at and what I need, shake his head lovingly as I pant uncontrollably and say, "Matthew just chill! Sit quietly with me. Breathe. Rest. Drink deeply. Disconnect for a while. Just come and sit in the shade, at my feet. Be still and at peace."

Are you tired? Worn out? ...

Come to me.
Get away with me and
you'll recover your life.

I'll show you how to take
a real rest.

Walk with me and
work with me —
watch how I do it.[18]

This morning an old Land Rover pulled up next to us as we were taking our morning walk. Mac had already entered sniper mode and he hit the deck as he had heard the vehicle approaching. He was alert, staring intently, ready for action. The driver? Well let's just say he looked like a stereotypical farmer: weather-beaten face, flat cap, old jacket, baggy nondescript trousers and, of course, green, mud-covered wellington boots. Opening the car door, he beamed at the sheepdog flat on the pavement in sniper mode, ready to round up the noisy metal beast. The farmer jovially said; "Ooooh. 'Eees good fer sheepin' – I'll take 'im off yer 'an's if you like!"

Clearly having experience with sheepdogs, the farmer had recognised that intense concentration and fixed stare and he was ready to take Mac up to his fields and put him to work.

I was tempted to ask how much he'd pay to take Mac off my hands, but as Mac looked up at me with those big brown eyes, I knew I couldn't.

Would my family ever forgive me if I came back from the walk with a pocketful of money and no dog?

I have read that farmers look especially for collies with a 'strong eye'. Collies with hard, staring eyes will notice if sheep are going astray and know to act. It is fascinating at times, to see Mac transform, in the blink of an eye, from a happy-go-lucky, trotting, sniffing family dog to a poised, alert, switched-on sheepdog. I just have to go near a sheep field and he goes into sniper/staring mode, seemingly trying to get sheep to move just by fixing them with his collie stare. It is said that many dogs demonstrate a form of ADHD[19] behaviour and we are experiencing this to be true of Mac. Border collies quickly become focussed on their task and even when they do rest, at least one ear and one eye is always alert. Mac seems at times to suffer from this sort of hyperfocus, when nothing, and I mean nothing, will make him take his gaze off a sheep — and don't even mention the word that shall not be uttered ... s-q-u-i-r-r-e-l. How can an animal that can be so fixated on one thing be so easily distracted at other times? If I were writing a school report card for Mac, I would write something like: 'Mac is a pleasure to teach, yet too often he can be distracted. If he could become as focussed and fixated on his work as he often is on other things, then he would become an excellent pupil.'

How is it that Mac can be so focussed on a task, showing workaholic traits, becoming compulsively fixated on what he perceives to be his task, and yet also be so easily distracted when I am trying to train him to learn something important or have him sit quietly at my feet? I realise that I, as the master, need to help him focus on the right things at the right times and not become so easily distracted at other times. I've found, for example, that scattering treats on the ground can distract him and get him sniffing and focussing on new things, or by just sitting and gently holding him close to me, I can settle him down and whisper in his ear, "*in ... rest you shall be saved, in quietness and trust is your strength.*" [20]

What really challenges me, is that what I have written in the paragraph above, about not being too easily distracted and focussing on the right things, would appear to be pretty good advice also for me, in my life. Sheepdogs are bred to be completely focussed on their task and to not be easily distracted, to never lose sight of the sheep: the task at hand. I increasingly recognise that for me, this is also vitally important. I realise that whilst it is good to be focussed, I need to ensure that I'm focussed on the right things in life. There are just too many rabbits and squirrels in the world that can lead me astray and have me fixating on the wrong paths.

> **Turn my eyes from looking at worthless things; and give me life in your ways.** [21]

I have just sat down to write this section. The setting is idyllic. A beautiful day, laptop on knees, lounging in a little seating area we have made at the top of our garden next to the pond. I probably won't be able to get much work done with Mac around, but I reckon I'll give it a go. If I'm writing about Mac and his relationship with me, the master, then what is better than to

*have my beautiful, obedient dog lying
at my feet as I type? A few doggy snacks
ready to bribe him to remain close, a nice
apple for me to munch and the laptop
battery fully charged – here we go!*

*Well, the beautifully idyllic scene lasted
all of 30 seconds before Mac heard a car
and headed for the front garden. I cannot
see him from my vantage point here, next
to the pond, so I had to go and get him
and make sure he's not digging up one of
Helen's flowers or found a hole in the fence
and decided to round up every car, cat and
person in the village.*

*So, I have returned with Mac on his lead,
a comfy blanket for him to lie on and a
pocket full of treats. He seems to be in more
of a playful rather than snoozy mood but
surely on this hot day he'll be happy to
settle in the shade for an afternoon nap
at the feet of his master? We've had our
morning run, Mac, now it is rest time.*

*Two minutes. It just took two minutes!
After some bribery and being tied to my
chair, he was just nodding off when he
opened an eye and saw a stick just about
within reach. A few minutes of distraction
and chewing and he seems fairly satisfied
and settled again.*

OK, so he's not actually sleeping, but at least he seems content to be close to me and sort of resting.

The stick soon became boring, so he turned his attention to some discarded pondweed which is just about in reach of that long tongue. Surely that's not tasty Mac? But it seems that it is even more interesting than one of his favourite treats.

I decide to take the pondweed away and try to get him to settle again. He looks at me, head on one side.

I tell him he has a choice, either settle here with me, or I'll take him back and lock him in his pen.

He looks at me, refuses to lie down and barks right at me. It's not a naughty or angry bark, just a 'come on, let's go and do something fun together' sort of bark.

He just doesn't understand that I want to write something really profound about his temperament, personality and his relation-ship with me, his master.

'Woof', another defiant exclamation, and I know it just isn't going to work. So we move: I set up camp, laptop right next to Mac's

favourite spot in the garden, where he can look out through the fence. He can watch the world go by and I am close enough to keep an eye on things whilst also typing.

Mac can hear the clicking of the computer keys and seems happy enough. However, when I stop typing and it goes quiet, he runs back a few steps from his vantage point and looks at me. He's just checking I am still here, that I haven't left him all alone. Must keep typing! Mac is content and feels safe, independent yet close, not feeling the need to spend the afternoon sitting at my feet but happy enough to know I am close by.

I don't think we consciously chose a dog that physically resembled us. However, when I consider Mac's temperament and traits as a Border collie, I wonder whether we somehow chose a breed that reflects somewhat on my, on our family's, rhythm of life and my natural inclinations? I recognise just how easy it is for me to have a mind addicted to adrenaline distraction: 'there's another ping from my social media, let's just check my emails, I wonder what has happened in the news in the last ten minutes, that YouTube clip looks interesting, what will the weather be like tomorrow, ooh there's an interesting new series on Netflix!' When I get a sniff on, it's amazing just how focussed yet distracted I can become all at the same time. Perhaps I need a short, sharp pull on the collar sometimes, just to snap me back to reality and help me to focus on what is really the most important thing. Perhaps I also need a master to force me to focus, and at times to stop and rest and just to be.

'Mac you just need to chill; learn to settle and don't take everything quite so seriously, especially when you are focussing on things that will lead you astray. When you are with me you can relax, I'll look after you, you can rest in my presence, just learn to settle down.'

Be still and know
that I am [the Master].[22]

CHAPTER 7

Sheep's poo

*Last night Mac followed my older son
into the downstairs shower room. Before
anyone had realised what was happening,
he (Mac, that is) had drunk all the water
from the toilet bowl.*

Now what is that all about?

*Why would our dog prefer drinking dirty
bacteria-ridden water from a toilet rather
than the nice fresh water that is in his very
own special bowl in the kitchen?*

*While we're on the subject, why is Mac so
fascinated with trying to eat sheep's poo in
the fields around our village when we offer
him nutritious, healthy food every day –
and if he is truly beginning to resemble me,
his master, what does this poo-eating habit
say about me?*

Once again there is that frustrating mirror that keeps
following me around, woofing at me when I don't give it
enough attention.

Is it possible that there are similarities between Mac and
me in our eating habits?

I think of the healthy foods, salads, fruit and pure water
I have on offer to me and consider how my diet too often
consists of rubbish – processed foods and sweet fizzy drinks.

But it's all just so tasty and tempting!

"What is that smell?"

We have just been out for the evening. Mac was safely locked away in 'his' room and yet there is an indescribable stench seeping through the house.

We checked on Mac and found a rather forlorn, guilty-looking dog, cowering in his bed, an egg box ripped apart on the floor and the remains of what must have been at least eight eggs on the floor and partially caked on his chin. He had somehow got hold of the egg box and helped himself. Raw eggs – yummy!

It is very clear from the resultant smell that raw eggs are not healthy for dogs. Putrid, decaying, rotten eggs mixed with sulphur and dead fish is probably the best I can manage to describe the stench that permeated through the house – and it lasted for days! The problem wasn't just Mac's natural exhaust. The smell seemed to seep out of every part of him.

He hasn't been allowed in the house for days, we had to wash all his bedding and the walls in the utility room – the stench penetrated everywhere.

I think we need to fumigate!

There are clearly some foods that look appealing and enticing but can really cause problems to an undisciplined dog or human. If we're not careful, it is easy to be drawn towards, and tempted by, a whole box of raw eggs, but we know from painful experience that soon stomach pains, nausea and rotten stinks can kick in.

Now, I personally do not have a thing for raw eggs or indeed for drinking from the toilet. I am however frequently enticed by pizza, cheeseburgers, fried chicken, chips, chocolate brownies and lemon meringue pie. Quite honestly my list could go on and on. There are simply so many foods that I fully understand are not particularly healthy, and yet so often I just cannot stop myself. Last weekend, settling down to watch a movie with the family, I could have chosen to snack on fresh fruit and a handful of nuts, or chocolate buttons, jelly babies and toffee popcorn – hmmm – it really was no choice!

As I reflect upon Mac's, and indeed my own dubious choices when it comes to the food we are drawn to, I think beyond the choices I make in filling my stomach and consider a wider question of what else I consume. How often am I tempted to fill my time with the triviality of all life has to offer? I could spend my free time reading a good book, having a positive, uplifting conversation with a friend, enjoying exercise and sports, pausing on a walk to take in the beauty of creation and generally filling my mind with wholesome and edifying things. Or, instead, I can insatiably consume rubbish on TV and streaming platforms, get hooked on social media, YouTube and all the internet has to offer, and demonstrate an unquenchable appetite to be entertained and distracted.

It's so easy to succumb, allow my life to be filled with trivial rubbish and be dulled into an almost comatose existence of hedonistic pleasures.

Surely there is more to life than this?

Observing Mac's choices forces me to ask whether what I fill my mind with is always the healthiest for me and whether the way I spend my time is actually, deep down, the way I want to, and should be, living my life? Perhaps Mac, with his fascination with toilet water, raw eggs and sheep's poo, has more in common with me than I care to admit.

> **Summing it all up, friends,
> I'd say you'll do best by filling
> your minds and meditating on
> things true, noble, reputable,
> authentic, compelling,
> gracious — the best,
> not the worst; the beautiful,
> not the ugly; things to praise,
> not things to curse.[23]**

But it's all very well saying I wish I could live a healthier, more balanced life both physically and emotionally. It's easy for me as I write this to try and motivate myself to 'do better', live a healthier lifestyle, make the right choices in what I consume and how I feed and fill my body and mind. The problem is, I seem to have a natural inclination, a compulsion, to act in a certain way, to think in a certain way and fill my life with unhealthy things.

Sometimes I just cannot help myself; I just don't have the willpower to change.

I cannot do it on my own.

I realise that I don't have what it takes. I can will it, but I can't do it.

I decide to do good, but I don't really do it; I decide not to do bad, but then I do it anyway.

My decisions, such as they are, don't result in actions.

Something has gone wrong deep within me and gets the better of me every time.[24]

We decided yesterday to address the issue of Mac frantically barking up the stairs and even guarding and trying to stop people from going up or down.

Now I am sure there is an element of his natural herding instinct kicking in here. He just wants everybody to be together in one room and if his 'sheep' escape upstairs then he has failed as a sheepdog.

We have not had the energy to try and address this, until yesterday, and recognise that this inbuilt bad behaviour, if not dealt with, will cause much frustration for us all and make home life pretty stressful. We know if not addressed, this bad behaviour could spiral and be much harder to address later on (old dogs, new tricks and all that) when it is even more ingrained in Mac's daily routine.

We're hoping that some 'distraction therapy', rewarding for not herding and barking, and the gentle, firm command and presence of the master will eventually help Mac overcome this errant behaviour.

Surely with our help he can overcome and change this behaviour that he just doesn't seem to be able to shift on his own – all we need is the patience to persist.

Border collies are natural herders. We see this instinct demonstrated in Mac when we are out on a walk and he sees pretty much any movement – be it another dog, a sheep, bird, car, c-a-t or s-q-u-i-r-r-e-l. At any movement, Mac naturally tenses and goes into alert mode. He quickly crouches low, ready to shoot off in order to bring the strays back into the herd. When a car goes past, and Mac is lying at my feet in alert mode, I often get a smile and a friendly wave from the driver. I sometimes see the occupants of the car pointing and imagine them saying, "Oh how cute; wow, that dog is so well behaved, look how he lies so still at his master's feet."

They have no idea!!!!

I would love to be able to say that Mac's prostrating himself at my feet is down to my incredible dog-training skills – but it's not. Mac is lying at my feet because that is what comes naturally to him as a collie when he sees movement (this is just before he feels a seemingly uncontrollable and irresistible urge to lunge at the car as it passes). Something deep within Mac, a natural instinct or compulsion, tells him to hit the deck and be alert because something is moving, and he may be required to chase and stop it. Whilst cute and fun to see, at times, this strong instinct is not always good and helpful for a domesticated family pet. It is, for example, hard to walk next to a busy road holding onto a strong, hairy monster who believes he is on a mission to stop (or at least chase/lunge towards) every car that passes.

Mac finds it difficult to rest when the whole herd/family are not all together in the same room. He finds it hard to control himself from guarding the stairs, not wanting to let 'sheep' escape upstairs or into the bathroom without him. It seems he feels a burden and sense of responsibility to live his life according to the deeply ingrained habits of centuries of breeding. Something deep within him tells him that he just has to try and keep us together. And so this strong, irresistible herding instinct manifests itself in Mac's barking up the stairs, interchangeable lunging at or prostrating before cars and his inner urge to chase and try to stop anything that moves.

I understand these deeply rooted, ingrained behavioural patterns are a part of Mac's nature and sometimes wonder if he will ever learn and change. Mac is no longer a sheepdog; he doesn't need to live according to those deep-rooted inner desires. He has a new life now; he's part of a new family, and some of those natural collie inclinations are unhelpful, unnecessary and cause much stress now that he has a life far away from his old farm. Those instincts and behavioural traits need to be overcome if he is to live a fulfilled, happy and peaceful life in his new home as part of a new family.

Mac has been adopted into a new family where he isn't required to hunt or round up sheep and chase things. Instead, he is invited to enjoy long walks, run and, yes, he can still enjoy running and chasing but can he learn that frisbees and tennis balls can be as much fun as woolly animals?

The problem is it just seems so difficult and unnatural for him to change.

Is there any hope for him?

As his master I sometimes crouch next to Mac when I see him in full alert mode. Maybe he has spied a s-q-u-i-r-r-e-l through the window, or someone has said a word that sounds like garage, and he thinks Helen is going to the garage to feed the c-a-t-s. Perhaps someone has just 'escaped' into the bathroom and Mac feels he has to be on full alert, lick the door a few times and prepare for rounding everyone up again. Or there's a pigeon perched on a branch of a tree and Mac believes it is his job to keep the garden free from all birds and ... well the list just goes on and on.

I sit next to the poor, desperate dog at these times and tickle his ears and whisper to him to calm down and relax: "Mac you don't need to worry about those things. It's all OK. You don't need to live with all this stress. I'm here, it's OK. Just relax. You're not required to live life like that anymore. Lie down boy. It's OK. I'm here with you."

Mac needs a master. Someone to just come alongside and guide him and hold him and comfort him. He needs help to remain calm and relaxed when something deep within him is urging him to run! Mac cannot overcome these urges on his own – we both know that he needs the steady, reassuring hand of the master.

Today Mac went 'self-employed'.

It's a beautiful morning and he wanted to go out into the garden.

I was doing some things around the house so left the door open and he shot out to do what he does.

Did he sniff and run around and explore and enjoy himself and snooze in the shade of a tree?

Nope!

For the last two hours, Mac spent his time staring at the chickens through the fence, trying to move them with the force of his

*collie stare. For minutes on end, he lay
frozen in sniper mode not moving a muscle
and then suddenly he would launch
himself at the fence. Every few minutes,
when hearing a car approaching down the
lane, he would run crazily along the fence,
seeing off the potential intruder before
returning to his chicken-staring vigil.*

*When I went outside Mac was very happy
to play frisbee and tuggy and generally
enjoy time with the master. But every time
I went back into the house, every time the
master was not giving him something
to do, he would feel the need to 'employ'
himself. He just couldn't stop, he had to be
doing something 'useful'.*

Mac needs the master to help him to understand, accept
and enjoy his new life. I am seeing that he simply cannot
change on his own, he needs the presence and oversight of
the master.

The natural traits and instincts, inbred within Mac, are
not of course wrong. These are traits, bred through many
generations of collies, set deep within him and they are mostly
behaviours that are helpful for a working dog. It's just that
in his new home and family Mac doesn't have to 'work' any
more. He would be happier and more content if he understood
that he no longer has to act and live according to those old
instincts, he has a new life now.

If anyone is [with the Master]
the new creation has come:
the old has gone,
the new is here! [25]

As I reflect upon these traits that I see Mac struggling to overcome, I find myself reflecting upon my life and asking whether there are any deeply ingrained behaviours in me that I also struggle to overcome in my own strength. I think of the (un)natural instincts and deeply ingrained flaws that battle for influence and control in my life. I may not have the inbuilt herding instinct of a Border collie, but I do recognise certain selfish traits in me that manifest themselves in the way I use my time, make priorities, interact with others and try to muddle through, live my life independently, go 'self-employed' and seek desperately to 'get outside', go it alone and separate myself from the Master.

When sitting or lying at my feet, Mac can appear to be calm, obedient and content, but I can tell when he is in 'alert mode'. I can sense when he is ready, in an instant, to lunge, or shoot off and use someone's stomach as a parkour trampoline to get to wherever he suddenly feels the desperate urge to be. To someone who doesn't know Mac, or indeed Border collies, it may seem that he's got it all together, is perfectly behaved, completely in control, happy and content; but what cannot be seen is that, too often, beneath that hairy black-and-white exterior, is a stressed, restless, struggling little dog who just needs to feel the steady, reassuring hand of the master and know that he is safe and loved, accepted and cared for; that he doesn't need to keep following those urges from deep within that lure him away from resting in the presence of his master.

Mac lies beside me. I reach down and gently touch him on the back and whisper, "Good lad, that'll do, settle down". He looks up at me, those big brown eyes searching for reassurance and then with a satisfied sigh he drops his head back on his paws and returns to his rest.

Wouldn't it be wonderful to experience in our lives a steady hand upon our shoulder when we need reassuring? To feel that we are safe, at home with the Master, knowing that we are held securely, that we don't need to constantly be on the edge, stressed, not understanding how we should be living our lives and worried about what the future may hold?

But who can help me somehow deal with my insecurities?

Who's going to help me deal with those deeply ingrained issues of selfishness that manifest themselves so often in so many ways?

Am I destined to spend my life drinking from the toilet, chomping on sheep's poo and stressfully thinking I need to guard the stairs for the rest of my life?

My deeply rooted desire to live independently, my natural inclination to be selfish with my time, my life rather than thinking first of the needs of others; all the consequences of this self-centred living, manifested in my, indeed all of our lives, are described in the Bible as sin.

*... the power of sin within me
keeps sabotaging
my best intentions,
I obviously need help!*

*I realise that I don't have
what it takes.*

I can will it, but I can't do it.

*I decide to do good, but
I don't really do it;
I decide not to do bad,
but then I do it anyway.*

*My decisions, such as they
are, don't result in actions.*

*Something has gone wrong
deep within me and gets
the better of me every time.*

*It happens so regularly
that it's predictable.*

*The moment I decide to do
good, sin is there
to trip me up.*

*I truly delight in [the Master's]
commands, but it's pretty
obvious that not all of me
joins in that delight.*

*Parts of me covertly rebel,
and just when I least expect
it, they take charge.*

I've tried everything
and nothing helps.

I'm at the end of my rope.

Is there no one who can do
anything for me?

Isn't that the real question? [26]

The quote above is how one of the writers of the New
Testament, the Apostle Paul, described his internal struggles
with selfish living. This is how he described that constant
urge we know so well to 'drink from the toilet bowl' and
chase after things that the Master says are not healthy for
us to chase after.

... we've compiled this long
and sorry record as sinners ...
and proved that we are utterly
incapable of living the glorious
lives God wills for us... [27]

Paul wrote about trying in his own strength but not being
able to overcome the natural inclination to rebel and turn away
from the Master. He wrote about delighting in the Master's
commands and yet constantly being 'tripped up' by sin.

We hear, and perhaps can identify with, the cry of Paul's
heart:

Is there no one
who can do anything for me? [28]

Isn't this the deep 'life question' that we all need to ask at some time?

Can I ever find true inner peace?

Can I ever find freedom and be set free from the inner conflicts, temptations and that deeply rooted selfish behaviour that the Bible describes as sin?

Are we destined to face a trudge through life, resigned to distracting ourselves into oblivion, hopelessly searching for something that hovers tantalisingly just beyond our grasp?

Is there no one who can do anything for us?

> **The answer, thank God, is that Jesus Christ can and does.**
>
> **He acted to set things right in this life of contradictions where I want to serve God with all my heart and mind, but am pulled by the influence of sin to do something totally different.**[29]

God, as the Master, understands our need; our inner turmoil, our struggles, and that sense of being tempted and pulled in different directions at the same time. He understands our battle with the selfish, sinful behaviour that we just cannot seem to overcome in our own strength. He understands the deep longing for peace and fulfilment, the yearning for true life that seems to be just beyond our reach.

That's why the Master sent his Son Jesus, the Christ (God's chosen and anointed one), to live among us. Jesus, God's Son, was the 'perfect man'. Living some two thousand years ago, Jesus's life, teaching, death and resurrection are described in the gospels at the start of the New Testament in the Bible. Jesus was crucified on a Roman cross having been unjustly accused of leading a rebellion. He upset the religious leaders of the day because he challenged their thinking and way of 'doing religion'. Jesus, having lived as a man, understands the weaknesses we all experience as human beings, because he himself was tempted in every way and yet he lived a sinless life.[30] By dying, Jesus took upon himself the punishment that our selfishness and sin deserves, and by rising to life, Jesus defeated death and demonstrated that new, resurrected life is possible.

In Jesus Christ there is hope for us all.

Since we've compiled this long and sorry record as sinners … and proved that we are utterly incapable of living the glorious lives God wills for us, God did it for us.

Out of sheer generosity he put us in right standing with himself.

A pure gift.

He got us out of the mess we're in and restored us to where he always wanted us to be.

And he did it by means
of Jesus Christ.[31]

God, the true and perfect Master, working in and through his Son Jesus Christ, is the only one who can help us overcome those deeply ingrained behavioural traits, the 'sins' that hold us captive to selfish behaviours that we just cannot shift on our own. Only by submitting to the Master and accepting his solution to our problem can we be freed to live as he intended us to live.

"This is how much God loved the world: He gave his Son, his one and only Son.

And this is why: so that no one need be destroyed; by believing in him, anyone can have a whole and lasting life.

God didn't go to all the trouble of sending his Son merely to point an accusing finger, telling the world how bad it was.

He came to help, to put the world right again."[32]

It doesn't make sense that Mac should choose to drink from the toilet and eat sheep's poo instead of the fresh water and healthy food that we provide for him. It would be crazy for a domesticated dog to insist on chasing after an independent lifestyle of rebellion, ignoring all the good things the master offers him.

In a similar way, we also can choose to continue to reject and live in rebellion against the Master. We can snap at him, fight, try to bite through the lead and run away, separating ourselves further from him, persisting in trying to go it alone.

We surely know, in theory, that it is healthiest if we are about the Master's business, not living in rebellion and not succumbing to those old habits and deeply ingrained behaviours.

It's not pretty when we try to go it alone and it usually ends in a mess.

Because living independently from the Master is not how he has created us to live.

God, the Master, loves us and he knows what is best for us, how to protect us and how to provide for us.

He knows when we need to work and when we need to rest.

The Master knows ...

> **"I know what I'm doing.**
> **I have it all planned out —**
> **plans to take care of you,**
> **not abandon you,**
> **plans to give you**
> **the future you hope for."**[33]

Two squirrels are scampering around on the grass; Mac's nemesis, the pigeon, is still threatening to leave the tree and land in the garden; a cat peeks over the fence; the chickens are strolling around their pen without any semblance of order, and cows are visible through the hedge, mooching about in the field next to us.

Mac looks up at me imploringly, desperation in his eyes. "I know you don't want me to master, but I just feel the urge to run and chase and herd them all – I just cannot help myself. What can I do? Help me!"

Give up.

Yield.

Submit.

With a long sigh just accept and be with the Master.

Accept him. Stop running off. Stop thinking the grass is always greener somewhere else. Stop eating poo when nutritious, wholesome, healthy food is available every day.

The Master loves us. He knows what is best for us and invites us to come to him. He alone can give us that deep internal rest that we so desperately need.

Now God has us where he wants us, with all the time in this world and the next to shower grace and kindness upon us in Christ Jesus.

Saving is all his idea, and all his work.

All we do is trust him enough to let him do it.

It's God's gift from start to finish![34]

CHAPTER 8

So why bother?

Our lives would be easier if we had never got a dog!

There, I've said it.

I have just witnessed Helen return from a morning run with Mac. It may have been dry when they left but let's just say they both looked a bit damp when they returned. Drowned rat is probably actually the best description – and I'm not talking about Mac!

Mac seemed chirpy enough, waggy and bouncy and happy to see me; Helen on the other hand, not so 'waggy'. She just looked at me, squinting through bedraggled, sodden hair. I decided against a cheery 'Raining a bit, is it love?' and concluded that silence was the best approach as she removed her trainers and squelched towards the shower.

I started this book with the question Why on earth would anyone want a dog? And that question is still hanging in the air like one of those smells that emanates from Mac when he lies in front of the fire and (over-)relaxes with us in the evening.

Through this book I have shared some of the frustrations, challenges, costs (financial, time, asthma, yanked arm muscles, clogged vacuum cleaners, etc.) associated with us being dog owners.

So, should we have got a dog?

Did we make a big mistake?

Why on earth would anyone want to own a dog?

What is the point?

Why bother investing significant effort and time into raising an animal that is not going to be around forever and quite frankly is costly and smelly and hairy and clumsy and sometimes is a real hassle?

It is early in the morning, and I am in the first days of planning this book, especially considering this question of 'What's the point of being a dog owner?'

I am sitting outside having a quiet moment of reflection and Mac just saw me. Helen must have just let him out of his pen where he has spent the night ... and he has just run at me.

He didn't run to me, but truly at me.

A bundle of crazed, frantic, hairy energy with a ridiculously long tongue hanging out of his mouth, he tore across the garden and skidded to a halt at my feet: crouching, wagging so much that he was bent in half, letting me pet him.

But that was not enough for Mac.

One jump, ready or not, and he is awkwardly lying across/on top of me literally trying to cuddle onto my lap and in my arms. I am not talking about a graceful, gentle leap, but a frantic jumping, scratching clamber, all hair, tongue, dog breath and bony elbows. He genuinely with utter abandon has jumped into my arms.

Trying to protect my book, my iPad and my groin area whilst a 24 kg hairy monster jumps on top of me is not easy. I am scratched and pretty uncomfortable, but I wouldn't swap that awkward, slightly painful show of affection for anything.

Sprawled half on top of me, Mac looks devotedly at me and gives me a little lick. I don't need the lick. I don't like dog slobber, but I know he is just trying to express and show his love.

I forget the cost, the asthma, the hairs, the smells, the bony elbows and even the slobber, because Mac is at home with me, he is part of the family and he just wants to be as close as possible to me, his master.

This routine is repeated pretty much every morning; Mac is let out of his utility-room bedroom and he hunts me down and comes running for a cuddle. It is always a bit awkward, front paws on my lap, not able to get comfortable, squirming around, he wants to get as close as possible, even before he has had his breakfast. He just wants to show his love and devotion.

Through the course of writing this book, as Mac has matured and calmed (slightly), his morning 'devotional' behaviour has developed slightly. He is not quite so frantic as he comes to me each morning. He still wags with his whole body and urgently pushes up against me, asking to be petted and reassured. A quick lick insists that my hands continue to tickle his ears when they stop. However, he is slightly more restrained now. He tends to sit at or on my feet, leaning heavily against my legs, just happy to be close, pushing up, leaning against his master.

For me, this morning behaviour, together with a similar reaction whenever we leave the house and return, partly helps answer my question 'Why would anyone want to own a dog?' There is something comforting about having a hairy, waggy friend who simply is always happy to see you and welcome you after even the briefest of absences.

Is this what makes owning a dog worthwhile?

Maybe, partly.

Yet, I suggest there is more to it than just receiving an awkward, uncomfortable doggy cuddle every now and again. I don't think my full answer is: 'It's worth owning a dog because it's nice for me as the master to receive devotion from him.' Yes, as a dog owner I happily receive that devotion from Mac, but maybe it is just as much that I have an object for my love and care as it is that I receive something from him.

I receive and have a devoted companion, but also, I am able to give and demonstrate love and care to one who receives with joyful abandon and seems to genuinely love to be close to me, have his ears tickled, tummy scrubbed, head patted and hear those whispered, affirming words: "Good boy Mac, good boy!" It's as if that is all Mac wants — that is all that he waits for every day. Mac lives to please his master and hear those comforting, reassuring words.

> **"His master replied, 'Well done, good and faithful servant! ... Come and share your master's happiness!'"** [35]

As I write this, Mac has been with us for nearly five months. He is now one year old and has gradually settled and become a part of our family. I have observed how frantic teenage energy and excitement is slowly transforming into loyal devotion. When he sits obediently and just looks up to me, his master, I see acceptance, willing obedience and devotion in his eyes.

Yesterday was a good day for Mac.

No, actually, it was a great day!

A morning run, the boys came home from school at lunchtime. TWO afternoon walks, including a special 'chase the ball at the park' walk – one of his favourites. TWO extra guests for dinner, and helping master bring wood to the wood burner in the evening.

The fire was so cosy and inviting that I couldn't resist lying down on the rug next to it rather than sitting on the settee – and Mac loved it. Some confused sniffing and licking was followed by snuggling, some awkward wriggling and finally following his master's example, with a deeply contented sigh, completely zonking out in the warmth of the fire – nose to nose (and I mean literally nose to nose) with me. Utterly relaxed, completely at peace, napping with the master.

Through these months, whilst spending time with Mac, I have had plenty of opportunity to consider my role as his master and I have continued to ponder the question that I began this book with: Is it worth all the hassle?

You will have noticed that I have often included verses from the Bible to illustrate and reflect upon that question in the light of our relationship as human beings with God, our Master. The Bible, God's Word to us, really does have the answers to all of life's deep questions. It's amazing that so few people actually take the time to read and search for the answers that so many of us are seeking.

These last months have caused me to recognise and, if truth be known, be somewhat shaken by my shortcomings as a dog owner. In chapter five I acknowledged that I am far from being the perfect master; this reality has led me to wonder what a perfect master would actually look like. My conclusion is that the best description of that perfect master is found in the many descriptions of God throughout the Bible. For example:

> ***[He is] a God of mercy***
> ***and grace, endlessly patient —***
> ***so much love,***
> ***so deeply true —***
> ***loyal in love for a thousand***
> ***generations, forgiving iniquity,***
> ***rebellion, and sin.[36]***

God truly is the perfect Master.

I wonder as I have written about Mac's experience of joining our family, whether you have reflected with me on how wonderful it would be, to be adopted into, and a part of, a loving and caring family, led and protected by someone who is always loving, gracious, patient, consistent and fully present; to be looked after and provided for by a master who actually wants to spend time with us and give us his attention; a master who, when we spend time with him, works with and in us, transforming us, helping us overcome those sinful, selfish habits that seem so ingrained in who we are.

My conclusion is that I don't want to go through life running wild, trying to be independent, living alone, lurching through life frantically chasing my tail. Deep down, I believe we all know that when trying to live without the Master, there is something missing.

*By taking a long and thoughtful
look at what God has created,
people have always been able
to see what their eyes as such
can't see: eternal power,
for instance, and the mystery
of his divine being.*

*So nobody has
a good excuse.*[37]

I recognise my need, I stop resisting and I acknowledge that I want, I need, to be close to a master who is always there for me, always leading, guiding and loving me unconditionally – a master who accepts me, knows what is best for me, who tells me when to rest; someone who will gently but firmly force me to stop and drink fresh water when I need to, and who will always, always, always be there for me when I am hesitant, lost or lonely.

[Master], my shepherd!

I don't need a thing.

*You have bedded me down in
lush meadows,
you find me quiet pools
to drink from.*[38]

*True to your word,
you let me catch my breath*

**and send me in the
right direction.**[39]

**Your beauty and love
chase after me
every day of my life.**

**I'm back home in the house
of [my Master]
for the rest of my life.**[40]

God, as the perfect Master, invites us to come to him; to 'sit by the fire' with him', to spend time in his presence, to be cared for, protected, provided for by him; to live with him, be adopted into his family and to experience him – maybe not exactly receiving tummy tickles; but to experience his firm yet comforting hand leading and guiding us through life, providing the security and reassurance that we all so desperately need.

This love and security are what God, our perfect Master, offers us. But why?

Just as I asked why would people want to own and care for a dog, can we not ask a similar question of God?

Why on earth would God want to look after and care for human beings?

People like me and you?

Why would God want to put up with, spend time with and be the Master of wild, rebellious human beings who continue to ignore, turn our backs and attempt to go it alone and live our lives independently of him?

> **We're all like sheep who've
> wandered off and gotten lost.**
>
> **We've all done our own thing,
> gone our own way.**[41]

What does God gain from spending time with, forgiving, accepting, providing for, and seemingly wanting to spend time with someone like me or you?

I've had first-hand experience of Mac's independent, wild, rebellious and deeply ingrained behavioural traits. I have endured the challenge, as his master, of seeking to train and see a transformation in him. It has, at times, been difficult and frustrating and only occasionally rewarding.

So why would God bother to reach out and offer to show love and transform self-centred, rebellious people like us?

Today I let Mac lead me.

We were walking through the woods and he was on his long flexi lead. Trails led off in many directions and rather than choosing one route and leading Mac, I let him choose and I simply followed along.

At one stage I looked ahead and saw that he was leading us in a circuitous route around a large tree. I thought of hauling him back onto my path and decided against it. Why not let him have some freedom, why not let him lead me? It really doesn't matter so much, I'm in no rush, let's just let him be and I'll follow along and enjoy just going a different way, walking at a different pace and experiencing a new perspective.

Then he saw or heard something; he pulled at the lead, wanting to leave the path. I could have pulled him back and forced him onwards, but I didn't. "What have you seen boy?" He looked up at me with that goofy smile, tongue hanging out and – was that surprise, excitement, joy in his eyes when I said, "Come on boy, let's check it out!"?

We both plunged off the path through the rough bracken towards the noise, Mac leaping ahead and leading the way.

It was nothing.

Or at least, by the time we had got there it was gone. But oh boy, did Mac enjoy taking me on that briefest of adventures – he jumped up excitedly, paws on my chest: 'that was fun, come on, let's do it again!'

*I loved seeing his doggy enthusiasm and
wagging tail as we returned to the path
and carried on.*

*We were together, he was with me, he
loved that I was fully present with him, and
he seemed really, really happy and ready
for another adventure – and so was I.*

At times, Mac pauses to smell something or moves in a
new direction, and as the master, I have a choice. I can choose
to pause with him, switch hands or spin and turn around, or
even follow him on a new path. Or I can roughly demand
that he stays close to me and stops dawdling and never truly
experiences the joys that are all around. I'm not suggesting
that God, our Master, follows us or that God changes his mind
when walking with us, but as I learn to walk with him as my
Master, it does appear that at times he patiently, lovingly,
caringly is willing to wait, wanting to engage with me. It
would seem that he really enjoys spending time with me!

As I walk with God, my Master, I grow more and more
accustomed to his voice. I hear and increasingly recognise
his commands, and sometimes experience a gentle, firm tug
when I have set off on the wrong path. However, there are
also times when it seems that he delights in allowing me to
choose the path or to hold back and enjoy the beauty of his
creation – just as long as I don't eat sheep's poo or run too
far from him!

Today Mac and I went for a walk.

We walked slowly down the lane – sniffing every blade of grass and peeing on bushes and gate posts as we passed (Mac, not me). No rush – just wandering on a beautiful spring evening with the master. Heaven!

I even let him lead me – I enjoyed it as I, to some extent, experienced the walk, the smells, the beauty, through his eyes and ears (and nose).

I noticed the frog that Mac woofed at, the leaf that gently circled to the ground and made him turn suddenly, the bird that warned others of our approach, the rustle of a squirrel or rabbit disappearing into the undergrowth.

I stayed close as Mac followed his nose down narrow trails – following the scent of badgers, foxes and other dogs.

I smiled as he kept turning back to me, checking I was there and apparently saying – "Wow – did you see that? Can you smell that? Listen! Can you hear what I can hear?"

I enjoyed, even revelled in, the beauty of all that we were seeing, hearing and smelling together. It was a beautiful day. I would have enjoyed the slow walk on my own, but being accompanied by and experiencing everything alongside Mac, sharing also in his joy, his excitement and waggy enthusiasm, somehow heightened the sense of enjoyment for me. It was special to experience something of Mac's joy, wonder and fulfilment as he experienced the manifold beauty of creation.

We came to a stile – it's quite a hassle for me to lug the hairy graceless lump up and over and then clamber over myself. But Mac was waiting for me and as I helped him over, he looked up and smiled a toothy, tongue-lolling, thank you as we set off together on the other side.

I could take this walk alone – in fact it would be easier with no lifting, no waiting, no peeing, no stopping and sniffing and running ahead and looking back longingly – but then there would be no shared experience and it certainly wouldn't be as enjoyable for me.

I love watching Mac enjoying himself, being happy and fulfilled; seeing him unworried, unrushed, just enjoying life in an unhurried, unstressed, happy way heightens my joy.

Our Master, Creator of the heavens and the earth, surely doesn't need all the hassle of looking after and caring for each of us. And yet, is it possible that he also enjoys, and is filled with joy by, spending time with us?

The whole Bible speaks of God's love for his people.

We read that "love is patient, love is kind";[42] again and again we see examples of God's love and patience for people whom he created, even when they (we) seem to continue to be wild, rebellious and 'untrainable'.

However, we do not just have a description of the Master loving people, we also read:

**... as a bridegroom rejoices over
his bride, so will your [Master]
rejoice over you.[43]**

I learnt at Sunday School the wonderful truth that God loves me. We've probably all heard that many times. But I wonder if I really grasped and accepted that he, God, also rejoices over me?

Wow, God rejoices over me! And he rejoices over you "as a bridegroom rejoices over his bride".[44] However, the 'honeymoon period' never finishes for God; he never tires of us, his love never grows cold, he is always enthusiastic and excited to spend time with us.

"Oh how I'll rejoice in them!

**Oh how I'll delight in doing
good things for them!"[45]**

He rejoices over each one of us – even when we insist on rolling in the mud, chasing after squirrels and turning our backs on him.

> **"The Lord your God is with you,
> the Mighty Warrior
> who saves.**
>
> **He will take great
> delight in you;
> in his love he will
> no longer rebuke you,
> but will rejoice over you
> with singing."** [46]

Now that is something to consider: God, as our Master, singing over us, rejoicing over us!

I think of a proud dog-owner bragging about how wonderful, good-looking, intelligent and obedient their dog is (I'm not quite there yet with Mac!). And that is the picture we have of God as our Master, rejoicing over us, rejoicing in us, not just tolerating our presence, but actually loving being with us.

When I accept this ... then I may be able to stop pulling on the lead and simply enjoy being with my Master.

When it feels that the Master is skipping along beside me without a care, fully engaged and enjoying life together with me – well, that truly transforms me and my outlook on life.

There is one who wants to be with me and with you, always close and loving, caring and forgiving. This extraordinary truth melts my heart, bends my will towards his and makes me feel utterly stupid and repentant for those moments when I run off and eat sheep's poo. Because I know, I just know that the Master is holding on to me and knows what is best for me.

"I know what I'm doing.
I have it all planned out —
plans to take care of you,
not abandon you,
plans to give you the future
you hope for."[47]

I love it when Mac is happy and contented, enjoying a morning run, fully alert, fully alive, running free but never straying too far from me, his master. He runs off and explores but I love to see his wagging tail and floppy ears as he comes bounding back to me, over and over again. He never seems to tire of running back to me, tongue hanging out, giving me a goofy smile as he runs close, checks in and then bounds off again to explore. When I see that Mac is happy and healthy and loving his life — well, it makes me smile, it brings me joy.

It seems, from what we read in the Bible, that this is similar to how God feels towards us. God loves it when we are fully alive, living as he intended for us to live, enjoying the beauty of all that he has created, never straying too far from him, always checking back in with him and enjoying life in his presence. God created us to be his 'image bearers' in his world. It is when we are fully devoted to him that we truly bring him glory, (thanksgiving, honour, admiration and praise) by reflecting something of his love and life to the rest of his creation.

The glory of God is
[a human being] fully alive.[48]

CHAPTER 9

You choose

Imagine a family visiting a litter of puppies, with a view to buying one. For so long they have looked forward to getting a puppy, a new member of the family. The children are excited, arguing about which one is cutest. "I like the one with the white tail!" "I want the one with a patch on his eye!" "Daddy, please, please can we get the small one that is more cuddly?"

Imagine that family driving away from the puppies with an empty basket and entering a high-tech robotics store. They invest in a remote-controlled chassis, a set of animatronic legs and a plastic 3D-printed dog's head. They get home and put together the robotic kit, choose what colour to paint the fake head and connect their phones via Bluetooth to the robot dog. Surely this would be perfect for the family! You get a dog that you can call (via your phone) and who always comes: no disobedience, no hairs on carpets, no poo bags, no vet bills, no feeding (just plug it in at night for a full charge). The 'dog' could be programmed to sit nicely by the fire, return to its bed every mealtime, only bark on command, even go on walks if you choose the more powerful battery and larger-wheel package. Surely this would be perfect for the family? Dog-owning without the hassle and drawbacks.

Of course, this is a pretty ridiculous scenario. We know the family don't actually want this. They want the unpredictability, the puppy chaos, the messiness. They want the puppy that will learn to love them as it grows into a fully grown dog. They want the cold, wet, dark winter walks and the hair-covered carpets, even the evening gassy pongs (well maybe not quite those as well but we get the picture).

So, why would the family want a dog that doesn't always do everything it is commanded to do?

A dog undoubtedly adds mess, frustration, chaos and uncertainty to the family dynamic and yet they (we) are willing to put up with all the hassle and frustrations so as to be able to enjoy also those moments of devotion and fun. For every smelly poo and chewed phone charger there are those moments when the real dog (not some robotic fake version) will look up at its master and there will be a connection. The dog will say with its big eyes, "I love you. I love that you feed me. I love that you care for me. I love that you take me for walks. I love that you play games with me. I love that you let me use your stomach as a springboard. I love when you invite me to sit by the fire with you. I love when you just talk to me even though it often doesn't make sense to me. I even love that you care for me enough to discipline me. I hate the baths and the vet injections but even then, I somehow understand that these are important and as long as I am with you, I am happy."

As I write this, Mac is almost sitting at my feet. I am in the garden, and he is dozing under the trampoline. I'd love to say he is lying beautifully by my feet but he's not. If he was a robodog I'd have him resting his chin on my foot as I type away. But he isn't a robot. He is a big, hairy, clumsy, messy Border collie who does not always do what I want, when I want. However, he is happy just being close enough. OK, so whenever a car goes down the lane he jumps up and runs to the fence; he is so easily distracted, but he soon returns to his safe spot, close enough to me to make sure I'm still there and knowing that he is safe because he chooses to be with his master.

I have already reflected upon the question of why God puts up with us human beings. And not just that he puts up with us, but that it seems he actually wants to be close to us, to enjoy a relationship with us, even 'rejoices' over us. Why has God allowed us to have free will, when he knows we all keep turning away from him, that we just cannot help choosing that self-centred rebellious lifestyle? Why didn't God create us to be like robots, always being obedient, always doing what he says when he says and never causing him pain or sacrifice? Surely that would have been easier?

Well, it would have been easier in many ways for the family in my story above to just buy a robodog, but they of course don't just want the perfect, obedient 'dog' that always does what it is told. They want a real dog that can choose to be close and devoted — or not. They want a dog that sometimes nips and poops and leaves hairs and makes smells. They are willing for all of that because they know that the dog will learn to love them, be devoted and obedient (mostly) and that will make it worth it. It is worth all the hassle to be able to have a dog that chooses to love; a dog that can be cared for and shown love to.

And so, we return to God.

It would seem that God also is willing to put up with so much, in order to allow us the choice of following or rejecting. He was even willing to pay the ultimate sacrifice so that we could be adopted into his family.

**But God demonstrates
his own love for us in this:
while we were still sinners,
Christ died for us.**[49]

Our Master loved us so much that even when we were wild and rebellious and knowing nothing of the life he offers, he took action. God made a way so that we could live in a relationship with him. He was willing to go through all that pain and rejection and separation within the triune Godhead (Father, Son and Holy Spirit) himself, because of his extraordinary love for us. He really loves it so much when people – that's you and me – choose to follow and worship and glorify and live in a relationship with him, just as he created and designed us to.

**This is how much God
loved the world:**

**He gave his Son,
his one and only Son.**

**And this is why: so that no
one need be destroyed;
by believing in him,
anyone can have a whole
and lasting life.**[50]

It would have been so much simpler if we were all programmed to always do his will, the will of the Master – but God has given us free will and we can choose to follow, or reject, him and his plan for us.

As independent human beings, we can choose to remain in our adopted family, choosing to submit ourselves to our Master and learning what is expected of us in our new home; or we can run off, as free as a wild, rebellious dog, living off whatever we find to eat, peeing wherever we want, chasing squirrels and following any trail that our noses draw us to.

The Master does not force us to stay with him, but he rejoices when we choose to accept and, in faithful obedience and love, follow him; when we come to that point of understanding just how wonderful it is to be adopted into his family, to be provided for and protected and guided and at home with him.

Our Master is full of grace. He continues to show love and care for us even when we don't deserve it; even when we've followed our noses and got ourselves into trouble; even when we've drunk from dirty puddles and eaten sheep's poo instead of the pure water and the wholesome pedigree food that is on offer to us; even when we've succumbed to those deeply ingrained character traits and feel out of control, running around frantically chasing our tails.

Our Master sees when we need to be calmed, he sees when there is danger ahead. He knows when to gently pull us back onto the path if we start heading in the wrong direction. He smiles lovingly and helps us redirect our focus when we get fixated on the wrong things. It seems that it even pleases him when we just want to be close to him, awkwardly jump onto his lap and cover him with slobber.

Maybe, like a dog with his master, we too can learn to look to our Master with total and complete devotion. Maybe we can learn to love him, seek to live our lives in ways that are pleasing to him, recognising that he knows what is best for us and that he actually rejoices over us!

Once we start trusting and are willing to follow the Master, we can be set free, but this involves having our rebellious nature dealt with. We first need to get sorted out what separates us from our Master and his plans and purposes for

us. The broken relationship must be repaired and then the life
he has planned for us can begin.

> *Therefore, if anyone is in Christ,*
> *the new creation has come:*
> *the old has gone,*
> *the new is here!*
>
> *All this is from God,*
> *who reconciled us to himself*
> *through Christ...*[51]

So God has made a way that we, despite all our problems
and independent nature, can come into his household and live
as he intended us to live. We no longer need to be tied up,
but can instead begin to live the life of true freedom that the
Master created for us to live. We can live in close relationship
with him, in devotion to him, hearing his voice, loving him,
loving being with him, resting in the knowledge that we are
safe with him.

> *Come near to God and he*
> *will come near to you.*[52]

At some stage, when we first invited Mac into our home,
he had to decide if he was going to live with us and accept
me as his master. He could have fought against us, turned
his back on the food we offered, the bed we made for him and
the fun, fulfilling walks and runs we offered. He could have
even insisted on living an independent life, heading off on his
own to live off sheep's poo and wild pheasant, drinking water
from stagnant puddles. The problem is that 'out there' in

the world are farmers with guns and dangerous tractors and combine harvesters; fast-moving cars on busy roads; bacteria and canine parvovirus and a thousand other dangers and illnesses that Mac needs to be protected and vaccinated from. It's just not safe for him to be out there on his own, and quite honestly his life is so much safer, happier and more fulfilled because he has chosen to stay with his new family and turn away from his wild, natural instincts and receive training from his new master.

"Come, follow me," Jesus said,[53]

God delights to be our Master and he invites us to choose to follow him and accept his plans for our lives. He loves to spend time with us, even rejoicing with us and over us. He loves to teach us and help us to overcome all those negative, deeply ingrained flaws, thus becoming all that he created us to be. God loves it when we enjoy the beauty of his creation. He loves to walk with us and enjoy life together with us. He loves it when we experience the fullness of what it means to be human, to be his image bearer − being like him and reflecting him in the world.

But does the fact that he wants to be, offers to be and delights in being, my Master actually make him my Master?

What if I ignore him and refuse to submit to him?

What if I run away from him and live independently?

Is he still my Master if I continue to reject, growl and snap at him, refusing to allow him to come close to me?

The Master may search for me, he may even bring me back to him time and again. But if I continue to reject and go my own way — well, surely then I cannot really claim to be adopted into his family and expect to enjoy all the benefits of being under his guidance and protection?

Is God my Master if I never spend time with him or learn to lie at his feet?

Today Mac did a runner. He was off the lead in the local woods, saw a squirrel and that was that.

Crazily running back and forth, he had a wild, frantic, excited, desperate, almost possessed look in his eyes as he belted past me again and again.

I called to him, but he didn't want to stop; he couldn't stop, he was out of control.

After a minute or so of crazed running, he was gone ... and I mean gone.

I looked beyond the woods and saw just a small wire fence separating us from a field full of sheep.

Mac in this uncontrollable, frantic, wild mood could easily leap the fence and then ... I could just imagine him racing around, chasing sheep, trying to round them up.

I called and called – nothing!

The seconds stretched into minutes. Still nothing!

After a couple of minutes Mac appeared again, running desperately, and then he threw himself at my feet. I mean literally threw himself – on his back with all four paws in the air, the wild look melting from his eyes as he pleaded with me. He lay there in the dirt at my feet, not caring about anything around him. As he gazed with those big brown eyes at me, his master, he was panting uncontrollably, saying, "Sorry, oh, I know that what I did was wrong, I know I should've come back earlier; I heard you calling, but I couldn't control myself – help me, please tickle my tummy, forgive me, I'm so sorry, I promise, promise, promise I won't do it again. Please, please, just forgive me and tickle me and help me to overcome this desire that too often consumes me to run off and chase squirrels."

I didn't need to get angry or punish him. Mac knew what he had done was wrong. I don't want to reward bad behaviour but when I see genuine repentance, well neither do I need to scold him.

Mac promised not to do it again, rolled onto his back and showed me his tummy in submission and utter abandon.

I bent down and tickled that hairy repentant tummy.

If we claim that we're free of sin, we're only fooling ourselves. A claim like that is errant nonsense.

On the other hand, if we admit our sins — simply come clean about them – he won't let us down; he'll be true to himself.

He'll forgive our sins and purge us of all wrongdoing.[54]

Mac was disturbed by an unusual noise on the TV this evening. Someone was whistling and he got quite distressed. He couldn't understand where the noise was coming from and what it meant.

Walking to the TV he cocked his head on one side and listened intently, then started whining.

*He glanced at me questioningly and I
reassured him: "It's OK Mac, come here, lie
down, it's OK, I'm here, you're safe, come
here boy."*

*Mac trotted over, flopped at my feet and
I reached down and tickled his ears. He
closed his eyes as I whispered, "It's OK boy,
it's OK".*

God, our heavenly Father, our Master invites us to spend
our lives with him, in his family and to be at rest in his
presence. Do you hear his words: "It's OK, you're home,
you're safe."?

... *do not fear for I am with you;*

**Do not be dismayed,
for I am your [Master].**[55]

About the author

Having grown up in England, Matthew spent the first twenty-three years of his adult life working in Eastern Europe with Operation Mobilisation (OM), a Christian missionary organisation. Since relocating with his family to England, he continues to work with OM, encouraging people to get involved in Christian ministry in the UK and overseas.

Matthew is married to Helen, who also works with OM, and they have five children. His first book, *Missionary, Me?,* tells the story of how he was surprised to learn that God can use each of us to make him known in the world.

Matthew speaks regularly in churches, where he shares about his faith and encourages listeners to consider life's big questions. He loves spending time with his family, playing and watching football, gardening projects, motor-home adventures and, of course, running with his dog, Mac.

Follow Matthew on Twitter:
@MatthewSkirton

Email:
MacandMe2023@gmail.com

ENDNOTES

1 Job 12:7 (MSG)
2 The story of our early years living in Moldova is written in my first book: Skirton, M. (2014) *Missionary, Me?* UK: OM Books
3 Parkour is an athletic training discipline where practitioners attempt to get from point A to point B in the fastest and most efficient way — including running, jumping, swinging, vaulting and rolling
4 Ephesians 1:5 (NLT)
5 Isaiah 43:1b (MSG)
6 John 10:27 (MSG)
7 *www.hmv.com/blog/music/100-years-of-hmv-our-story-so-far*
8 Psalm 23:1–3
9 Psalm 16:1
10 Psalm 73:28a
11 Psalm 138:7 (AMP)
12 James 4:8 (RSV)
13 For example: Perina, K. 'Are we attracted to people who look like us?' Psychology Today [Internet] 2015 May 13. Available at: *https://www.psychologytoday.com/gb/blog/the-mysteries-love/201505/are-we-attracted-people-who-look-us*
Ducharme, J. 'Why Do So Many Couples Look Alike? Here's the Psychology Behind the Weird Phenomenon'

Time [Internet] 2019 April 4. Available at: *https://time.com/5553817/couples-who-look-alike/*

14   Robson, D. 'Dogs look like their owners it's a scientific fact' BBC Future [Internet] 2015 November 12. Available at: *https://www.bbc.com/future/article/20151111-why-do-dogs-look-like-their-owners*

15   For example: Leifler, K.S. 'Dogs mirror owner's stress' Linkoping University News [Internet] 2019 June 6. Available at: *https://liu.se/en/news-item/hunden-speglar-agarens-stress* Also: many articles found searching for 'Dogs reflect personality of owners'

16   Romans 12:2 (MSG)

17   Fear Of Missing Out

18   Matthew 11:28 (MSG)

19   Attention Deficit Hyperactivity Disorder

20   Isaiah 30:15 (AMP)

21   Psalm 119:37 (ESV)

22   Psalm 46:10a

23   Philippians 4:8 (MSG)

24   Romans 7:18–20 (MSG)

25   2 Corinthians 5:17

26   Romans 7:20–24 (MSG)

27   Romans 3:23 (MSG)

28   Romans 7:24b (MSG)

29   Romans 7:25 (MSG)

30   Hebrews 4:15

31   Romans 3:23–24 (MSG)

32   John 3:16–17 (MSG)

33   Jeremiah 29:11 (MSG)

34   Ephesians 2:7–8 (MSG)

35   Matthew 25:23

36   Exodus 34:6 (MSG)

37   Romans 1:19–20 (MSG)

38   Psalm 23:1–2 (MSG)

39 Psalm 23:3 (MSG)
40 Psalm 23:6 (MSG)
41 Isaiah 53:6 (MSG)
42 1 Corinthians 13:4
43 Isaiah 62:5
44 Isaiah 62:5
45 Jeremiah 32:41 (MSG)
46 Zephaniah 3:17
47 Jeremiah 29:11 (MSG)
48 attributed to Irenaeus (a leader in the early second-century Greek church), *Adversus Haereses, book 4, chapter 20*
49 Romans 5:8
50 John 3:16 (MSG)
51 2 Corinthians 5:18–19
52 James 4:8
53 Matthew 4:19
54 1 John 1:8–9 (MSG)
55 Isaiah 41:10